COLLECTING
AMERICAN
FOLK ART

COLLECTING
AMERICAN
FOLK ART

Helaine Fendelman and Susan Kleckner

HOUSE OF COLLECTIBLES

NEW YORK

House of Collectibles and colophon are registered trademarks of Random House, Inc.

RANDOM HOUSE is a registered trademark of Random House, Inc.

This book is available for special discounts for bulk purchases for sales promotions or premiums. Special editions, including personalized covers, excerpts of existing books, and corporate imprints, can be created in large quantities for special needs. For more information, write to Special Markets/Premium Sales, 1745 Broadway, MD 6-2, New York, NY, 10019 or e-mail specialmarkets@randomhouse.com.

Please address inquiries about electronic licensing of reference products for use on a network, in software or on CD-ROM to the Subsidiary Rights Department, Random House Reference, fax 212-572-6003.

Visit the Random House Web site: www.randomhouse.com

Library of Congress Cataloging-in-Publication Data is available.

First Edition

10 9 8 7 6 5 4 3 2 1

September 2004

ISBN: 0-375-72051-0

CONTENTS

FOREWORD

As a field in the history of American culture and art, American folk art is relatively new. To be sure, it has been the subject of exhibitions and published studies for more than three quarters of a century, but its widespread popular appreciation is a phenomenon of more recent times. It is not surprising that American folk art speaks to us because much of it is deeply grounded in our shared heritage. Drawing from the wellsprings of American culture, folk art speaks to the creative gifts and technical virtuosity of artists who paint, sculpt, carve, construct, decorate, embroider, quilt, or build for the sheer joy of it, or who feel drawn to express themselves artistically through an inner calling or compulsion.

In view of the extent of the growth and development of the field of American folk art over the last two or three decades, newcomers inevitably find it difficult to marshal the considerable resources currently available to an understanding of the subject. Novice collectors invariably make costly mistakes, and budding scholars are bewildered by an increasingly diffuse and complex body of literature. A practical, introductory guide to the field has long been necessary.

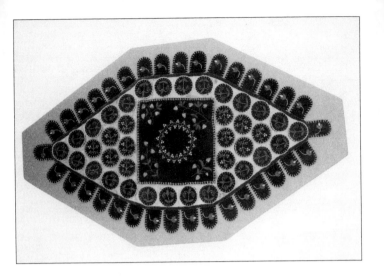

Penny Rug with Stuffed Strawberries
c. 1850–1860, Vermont.
In an elongated octagon shape made of wool, silk and metallic thread surrounding strawberries.
61" H × 38" W
Photo courtesy Ballyhack Antiques

As director of the American Folk Art Museum, I am delighted that Helaine Fendelman and Susan Kleckner—both of whom have been professionally involved in the field of American folk art for many years—have produced just such a work. Well known and highly regarded by collectors, dealers, and the community of scholarship alike, they have brought together in this volume a treasure trove of vital facts and references, and have provided helpful suggestions for the gathering of further information on all aspects of the subject. A true "instant expert" understands how much he or she does *not* know, and seeks advice from authoritative sources. Helaine Fendelman and Susan Kleckner not only suggest what questions to ask, but provide a comprehensive resource guide to accurate, reliable, and practical answers.

Gerard C. Wertkin, Director
American Folk Art Museum, New York

ACKNOWLEDGMENTS

The authors would like to thank their colleagues in the American folk art field for their generosity and support in completing this book. Whether fact or omission checking, their interest and commitment to this project have been invaluable; a special thanks to Kathryn Abbe, Nina Hellman, Frank Maresca, James Mitchell, John Ollman, Roger Ricco, David Schorsch, Penny Stillinger, David Wheatcroft, and Paula Laverty, our Grenfell scholar. To all who sent photographs, we are particularly indebted. Gerry Wertkin's summary of the enduring magnetism of American folk art and its challenges to new collectors eloquently sets forth the absence this book seeks to address. We salute our editor and friend Dottie Harris whose encouragement and vision are unparalleled. Kudos to Lindsey Glass, Dottie's assistant, for her aid. Finally, *Instant Expert: Collecting American Folk Art* would not have happened without the tenacity, efficiency, organizational skills, and dedication of Francie Mrkich.

On a personal note, we would also like to acknowledge gratefully the patience of our husbands, Burton Fendelman and Jonathan Goldstein.

Helaine Fendelman
Susan Kleckner
New York City and San Francisco, September 2004

INTRODUCTION

Many books about Americana or the art market address how to navigate the marketplace and not be fooled by cunning forgeries or enlighten about specific types of materials or specific collectors. No other "field guide," for that is what this book truly is, offers a comparative analysis between objects—why one example may be better than another. And no other book combines this critical analysis with a historical context for its readers. The latter is uniquely important to the Americana market, not only as a means of understanding why we collect the American folk art we collect, but also so readers can enjoy other collectors' experiences and know how they are part of an illustrious tradition.

Instant Expert: Collecting American Folk Art is comprised of eight chapters and an Appendix. Each chapter discusses a different aspect of this book, starting with its purpose—Chapter 1 defines what an instant expert is and why you need to be one. Chapter 2 talks about the objects themselves and attempts to provide a framework by which to understand what American folk art is. Chapter 3 discusses the European antecedents of American folk art. Chapter 4 narrates the history of the American folk art market, how it started, where it went, and the lessons of its most recent activity. Chapter 5 explains the record prices paid for American folk art at auction, who paid them, and why. Chapter 6 provides you some tools, both mental and physical, with which to assess objects, and Chapter 7 is an extensive database of resources—from museums to auction houses, antiques show promoters to collecting groups, conservation supply sources to publications; this chapter tells you how to access information. And since no course is complete without a final project or test, Chapter 8 is the Instant Expert Quiz to see how you've applied the information set forth here. While the answers to the questions are at the end of the test, the book up to Chapter 8 is the coursework that will provide you with most of the answers to Chapter 8 and undoubtedly many other American folk art mysteries. Finally, the Appendix gives you more ways to study beyond this book. In addition to a glossary of terms useful in describing American folk art, there is a brief annotated bibliography where you can find a few more titles with which to continue your quest. Some quiz answers lie in the Appendix, so feel free to read ahead.

Let the learning begin!

1

WHAT IS AN INSTANT EXPERT?

Whether it's a piece of pottery found at a flea market, a weathervane discovered at auction, or a sampler found at a yard sale, antiques add individuality to our homes and enrich our lives with the history they impart and the questions they inspire. Sometimes these questions are as basic as "What is it?" and move on to "Who made it?" "When was this used?" and "Who used this?"

With the popularity of television programs revealing glimpses of the antiques market, these questions are more often about rarity, price, and authenticity. "Did I pay too much?" "Did I find an unrecognized treasure?" "How unique is my antique?" and, most importantly, "How antique is my antique?" By becoming an instant expert, you will be able to answer these questions your-self and know when and where to turn for more experienced guidance.

This book intends to dispel some of the mystery surrounding a specific group of antiques: American folk art. Of all the collecting categories in the art market today—furniture, carpets, paintings, jewelry, and vintage clothing, to name only a few—American folk art is probably the most popular; it captures our imagination and affection for a simpler time. American folk art is easily understood, is the broadest ranging in its scope, and is among the most affordable to collect. The high prices paid for that small percentage of well-marketed, rare objects offered in the marketplace should not deter anyone interested in this exciting and rewarding field!

American folk art is also one of the most subjective areas of the art market and the most fraught with confusion. First, what is it? Second, unlike areas of the fine arts, there are few definitive catalogues raissones for American folk art; one generation's trash is another's treasure; one buyer's definition of American folk art is not another buyer's definition. Sadly, with some of the heftier prices paid for American folk art, this collecting category is not without forgeries as well. For these reasons, anyone interested in collecting this rich and inclusive material record of America's past needs to read this book.

What is an instant expert?
An instant expert is someone equipped with the eye to see quality, the mind to question the authenticity of the object, and the discipline to learn this field. Plenty of material available in the marketplace looks fantastic, but is it? By understanding the objects in front of you and learning what to look for, you can develop a discerning and critical eye so that you have a good idea of what you're buying and you know how and where to seek help when you don't. Expertise in a given connoisseurship area is never instant; this book will allow you, however, to begin to think and talk like an expert and jump-start your education.

Learning about antiques takes time, diligence, and applied study. While there are few greater teachers than the marketplace, take advantage of the expertise around you. Dealers, collecting societies, antique shows, auction house staff, and curators in your area hold a wealth of knowledge and most are happy to share their information. This book supplements your education by including a section on magazines and periodicals that relate to American folk art and its market. Be prepared to make some mistakes and recognize them for the learning opportunities they are—hopefully, you will never make the same mistake again and remember that even the most experienced experts are sometimes wrong!

Among the most important questions to ask with every object encountered are: "What's outside?", "What's inside?", and "Is it the best of its type?"

What's Outside?

"What's outside?" means two things.

First, it means the exterior. With most American folk sculpture, furniture, decorations, and paintings, the surface yields valuable information. Does the surface plausibly have the finish, age, accumulated crud (also called patina), and expected wear that an object of its purported age should have according to its alleged function? If it doesn't, why not, and how important is that absence to the value of the object? If the surface is painted, the same questions apply along with others: Does the paint indicate anything about the area of origin? Does that affect value? Is the paint old? Is there repainting? How much is repainted? How do you tell? How important are these factors relative to the value of the object? In the case of textiles, what is the latest era to which you can date a fabric (weave or pattern), a yarn type, or a color? The latest date of any of those variables is usually the earliest point at which that textile was made.

Second, "What's outside?" also means the narrative surrounding the object, whether purpose, provenance, or family history. Is the purpose plausible for the time and place in which the object was made? Understanding the era and culture that produced whatever form of American folk art interests you will put you in good stead for understanding specific examples. With these questions at your disposal, you will know immediately to be wary of forms that on reflection don't make sense, like an eighteenth-century American Chippendale sideboard or an Amish fraktur birth and baptismal certificate.[1] Provenance, or history of ownership, while sometimes fabricated (usually in instances where a larger fraud is at hand), can be a valuable tool in assessing the age of an object. If the object were in an historic auction or traceable advertisement, sometimes an identifying photo or further clue to the object's history is also published. In the case of an historical person, some record of that individual may still exist that also sheds light on your antique.

In some instances, family history can yield important leads in further identifying objects. Family traditions can also distract you from the detective work at hand and should be received with a dose of healthy skepticism. Sometimes a family legend grows grander over time; sometimes it relates to a previous owner rather than the object at hand, or it simply could not have happened. On more than one occasion, a needlework sampler has been presented for appraisal, proudly pronounced as having been made by an ancestor who came over on the Mayflower, yet worked in a style and from materials that did not exist in America until 1850. Family lore rarely adds value to an otherwise uninteresting object unless specifically relevant to the appearance or manufacture of the object in which you are interested. Part of being an instant expert is detective work, knowing how to sniff out fact from fiction and learning whether a discovery enhances your understanding or just leads you away from the truth.

What's Inside?
"What's inside?" means construction. Is the object put together in the way it should be for its time and place of manufacture? Knowing what materials, tools, and techniques were available at what time will tell you approximately

[1] By the time the sideboard came into use in American homes in the late eighteenth century, the "Chippendale" style, as it has come to be called, was already out of vogue. Accordingly, there is no such thing as an American eighteenth-century Chippendale sideboard; such an object would automatically be, in antiques-speak, "second period" or a reproduction. Similarly, an Amish fraktur birth/baptismal certificate is nonexistent as well: the Amish do not practice infant baptism.

when an object was made or when it was repaired. Since different types of objects result from different technologies, knowing when and how a manufacturing technique changed over time will guide you to the right approach to take with that object.

Paint Decorated Chest of Drawers
c. 1835–1840, Mahantango Valley, Schuylkill County, Pennsylvania.
Polychrome finish on a green and blue ground.
49" H × 44" W × 20" D
Photo courtesy David Wheatcroft Antiques;
Private collection

For example, most furniture manufacturing has changed dramatically in the last 200 years. Most pottery and glass making has changed comparatively less as their manufacture retains more traditional techniques. Accordingly, how you approach and assess these two types of objects relative to their construction will be determined by what material you would expect to see and the appropriate manufacturing techniques.

Pillow Top Windsor Side Chair
c. 1830, probably Philadelphia. With original white paint and decorated finish. 34" H
Photo courtesy Olde Hope Antiques

Best of Type

Assessing antiques in the marketplace requires the same discriminating sense you would use in any other purchasing choice; only your comparison pool is different.

Just as your choice of more everyday goods or services might be guided by the question "Is this the best of this type of product available to me?" the same question applies to antiques. Where does your specific antique objectively fit on the scale of its type? Is it a standard example? Is it a plainer example? Is it a rare example and, if so, why? What makes it rare and how important is that relative to your collecting goals? What is its condition? Being ruthlessly disciplined in your assessment of all the antiques you see will train your eye and allow you

Flag Quilt
[good example]
c. 1920–1930,
American.
Pieced quilt
with a series of
fifteen flags
stitched in three
columns of five.
Approximately
78" H × 76" W
Photo courtesy
Shelly Zegart

to make more confident, informed choices. This book will attempt to show qualitative distinctions, the "good, better, and best," among examples of American folk art so that you can better understand what's below average, what's average, and what surpasses the rest.

Bear in mind that, unlike a melon at the produce stand, the body of objects against which you will compare your antique is not right in front of you. Going to antique shows, museums, and dealers' shops is the first step to creating your own mental repository from which to compare the object you are considering to others of its type. Most importantly, joining your local library or museum/historical society, whose library may better suit your needs, will provide you with an invaluable source of illustrated material from additional public and private collections. Remember that rarity doesn't necessarily mean more valuable, and similarity to an object in a museum collection doesn't necessarily add value, either. If an object is a standard example of a commonly available form, then it is a standard example of a commonly avail-

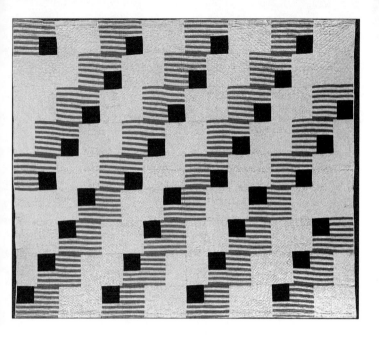

Flag Quilt
[better example]
c. 1920–1930, American.
Pieced quilt with a series of flag motifs stitched in alternating diagonal stripes.
Approximately 82" H × 62" W
Photo courtesy Shelly Zegart

able form regardless of who else owns one like it. Studying the literature of American folk art will provide you with a large measure of information to make that call for yourself.

This book includes an annotated bibliography of must-read titles to familiarize you with the richness and variety that is American folk art. This list is only a start: for as many different kinds of people that came to America, or were here already, there are as many different examples of American folk art. The bibliography is groundwork for further reading; in addition, each book has a bibliography of its own that can take you wherever you choose! By focusing on this point in more recent publications, however, you will benefit from the past expertise and scholarship on which these newer titles were founded.

Finally, it is also important to acknowledge that one person's best of type is not necessarily another's, and both conclusions may be valid. A very clear definition of interest will save you from overspending on what doesn't meet your collecting criteria, feeling good about stretching yourself for what does, being able to let something go when circumstances call for it, and knowing the dif-

Flag Quilt
[best example]
c. 1920–1930,
American.
Pieced quilt
with a central
flag motif
surrounded by
crosses set in a
diamond
border. Size
unknown
Photo courtesy
Shelly Zegart

ference among those three scenarios. In June 2003, a
rare example of a type of needlework produced in Boston
in the 1740s came to auction at Butterfield's in San Francisco. The needlework was large for its type (it was designed to hang over a fireplace mantel), it had some
losses, and the color was a little dark. Most unusual
about the needlework, however, was the presence of an
African-American woman in the center of the scene.
Women usually populated these needleworks, since they
were intended to depict courting scenes. Such an explicit
depiction of an otherwise significantly underrepresented
race, however, made this needlework highly unusual. Between this feature and its essential rarity overall, the
needlework was expected to sell well beyond its estimate
of $20,000–30,000. While some interested bidders were
collectors of high-end Americana and perceived the
needlework as an important work of art that filled a gap
in their collection, American needlework collectors ap-
praised Butterfield's offering differently. By auction's
end, the needlework sold for $611,250.

To the general high-end Americana collector, the needlework was worth comparatively closer to its estimate because it was the form in general that interested them, not the specific details and rarity of that object. The rarity of the one character in the picture was irrelevant to those collectors, so it was right for them to drop out of the bidding when the price became too high for their goals. To collectors and scholars specifically focused on American needlework, however, the rarity of the single central African-American figure redefined the work and placed it on the level of masterpiece. Only eight similar American needleworks are known, all are in museum collections and, therefore, are probably never going to be available in the marketplace. The example at Butterfield's was truly unique and easily worth just over twenty times the high end of the estimate.

The purpose of this book is not to intimidate readers with exceptional prices paid for rare examples of American folk art, but to teach readers how to navigate this group of antiques and its market. The reader will learn how to discern whether some objects are important whereas others are not; to understand why high prices are paid for some works but others are left unsold; to make reasoned and informed choices about works of art that can be as colorful and varied as the nation in which they were made. ◾

2

FACETS OF AMERICAN FOLK ART

American folk art is difficult to define: For every definition, there is at least one contradictory example. American folk art has been described as self-taught, nonacademic, or untrained work, in reference to those artists who were not formally schooled in their area of artistic production. Yet young girls in a seminary generally made needlework samplers and silk pictures; fraktur artists were often schoolmasters, and some media, such as base metals and pottery, required an apprenticeship. American folk art has been described as handmade, the result of individual effort rather than mass production. An entire category of weathervanes, one of the most immediately recognizable forms of American folk art, however, was factory made, as were some decoys and cigar store figures. American folk art has also been called primitive and naive, suggesting its graphic success is primordial and accidental. Whether an itinerant portrait, a memory painting or even a patterned quilt, the process of creating such work is rooted in decorative tradition and choice, neither of which is primitive or haphazard. In contrast, the term "outsider art" is more about the artist than the work, and as such may provide more accurate expectations for what the work is. Whether for medical or economic reasons, these artists exist and create outside the bounds of mainstream culture. Accordingly, their inspiration springs from alternative sources and is filtered differently from how these same stimuli might be received by someone living in more abled or empowered circumstances. Outsider art is generally regarded as a twentieth and twenty-first century phenomenon, though several giants of the outsider tradition were, in fact, born in the nineteenth century.

Whether the utilitarian, decorative, recreational or ceremonial tools of early everyday life, factory-produced goods or outsider art, these categories of American folk art reflect a people as diverse as the objects themselves. Nonetheless, these objects also share a binding resonance. They reflect common cultural heritage, community traditions, and the enduring importance of patriotism, religion, and popular culture in American life.[2]

What Is It? An Object and Maker Tutorial

The following list, by no means exhaustive, comprises an essential database of the different types of objects you will encounter, all of which are American folk art.

This section has been divided according to basic media (i.e., painting, sculpture, textiles, outsider art) with each successive sub-section first identifying media (oil on canvas, oil on board, watercolor, pastel on paper), then more specific purpose (i.e., portrait, landscape), and then the name of an artist who produced such works.

[2]One definition of American folk art as promulgated by the American Folk Art Museum.

It is important to understand that the largest group of makers and decorators in the field of American folk art are now, and probably will remain, anonymous. Most of what was made or decorated in the folk tradition in the eighteenth and nineteenth centuries was for one's self, a loved one, or one's own community, none of whom required a signature. The works were not considered important enough for the maker/decorator to put his or her name on the piece.

For objects by known makers, you should familiarize yourself with the names and output of those artists whose names have been included. The purpose of listing them is to provide you, in your own research, with a maker whose work will familiarize you with what is meant by each object. In some instances, you will see the same name twice: This is to underscore that most of these artists were working craftsmen or women who plied their trade through more than one medium. Also included in this book are photographs showing what most objects in each category are as well.

Painting
Genre
Genre and anecdotal painting roughly paralleled the emerging Hudson River landscape school of painting, which flourished in America during the middle of the nineteenth century. Hundreds of untrained artists celebrated scenes from everyday life. Though some paintings are mildly didactic, genre painters did not intend serious social reform, but served to record their surroundings.

Still Lifes
A still life rendering usually depicts flowers, fruits, vegetables, and foliage in bowls or within the home environment. These pictures were usually done in freehand style. One particular mode of the still life is tinsel pictures, a nineteenth-century parlor art form. They were pictures painted on glass and backed by crinkled tinfoil. Tinsel pictures were sometimes called crystal painting or Oriental painting and frequently depicted still life paintings.

A popular schoolgirl art form, as well as a creative outlet for adult women, was executed by using theorems, stencils arranged in pleasing designs and then painted.

Carved Figure of a Man Wearing a Top Hat and Tails, Dated 1938, Pennsylvania. Polychrome wood with jointed arms; signed underside of base "WH. Stephens Uniondale PA 1938." 15" H

Miniature Copper Tea Kettle, Late eighteenth century, Pennsylvania. 6 1/2" H

Paint Decorated Pine Trinket Box, Dated 1856, Pennsylvania. With lift-top lid and decorated with red and yellow pinwheels and the inscription "Presented to me by A.R. Taylor, September 27, 1856" on reverse "C.A.____," over a face with two red, yellow, and green philflots flanked by sides with red and yellow five-point stars, on brown ground with red borders. 3 3/4" H × 9 1/2" W Provenance: Descended in the family of William Poulson, Claymont, Delaware

Redware Charger, Mid-nineteenth century, Pennsylvania. With yellow slip decoration. 12 3/4" Dia.

Miniature Paint Decorated Blanket Chest c. 1860, Pennsylvania. Joseph Long Lehn (1792–1898), With a lift-top lid over a conforming rectangular case resting on turned feet, retains brown painted surface with red, yellow, and green pin striping and floral decoupage appliqués. 5 1/2" H × 8" W

Tin Teapot, Dated 1824, Pennsylvania. Oliver Filley Tinsmiths, inscribed on underside "H. Case, April 1824," With yellow bird and fruit decoration and some paint loss. Signed examples of tin are exceedingly rare. 11" H

Paint Decorated Walnut Apple Tray, c. 1850, Pennsylvania. With canted dovetailed sides on turned feet, retains an old ochre grain painted surface. 5" D × 10" W. Provenance: Henry Francis du Pont, Photo courtesy Pook & Pook

Frequent subjects for theorem paintings were still-life arrangements of fruit, flowers, and vegetables. Although tracing was a basis for the individual forms, the results were often not mechanical because the artist demonstrated a fine sense of color, design, and handling of the medium on paper, silk, satin, or velvet.

Fireboard

Most often paint-decorated in trompe l'oeil fashion, fireboard panels were executed on wood or on paper or canvas attached to wood. Used in summer months when the parlor fireplace was not in use, fireboards were useful for keeping small animals and soot out of the best room and served a decorative purpose.

Boxes

Wooden boxes are particularly appealing to collect because of their endless assortment in size, shape, and decoration. Decoration was in carved or incised, and/or painted form. Boxes that were hung commonly held combs, tableware, spices, or candles. Those that sat or stacked on tables stored other household necessities. Shapes were rectangular, round, oval, or square. Sometimes the boxes were left plain, but more often their form lent to the decorative whims of the maker. Paint-decorated boxes were popular, but their endless variety also included painted scenes, floral decorations, and personal inscriptions. Bible boxes (1700–1835) were primarily found throughout New England and Pennsylvania. A Bible box sported a flat or slanted top intended for use on tables or benches and held the Bible or other valuables. Slanted tops were used for writing. Oak or pine was used most often. Names to recognize are the Pennsylvania "Bucher" and Compass Artist boxes, Joseph Long Lehn, Rufus Porter, and Isaac Stiehly.

Architectural Ornaments

Typically, exterior building ornaments reflect patriotic symbols, fleur-de-lis patterns, or unusual grotesque faces or beings. These façade embellishments were made from a variety of materials including wood, stone, iron, tin, and concrete, and reflect the architectural trends of the times in which they were created. Commonly, most specimens found today date from the 1875–1925 period.

Paint Decorated Cupboard
Mid-nineteenth century, Saranac Lake, New York. Step-back cupboard with four recessed paneled doors and all-over multicolored paint decoration, originally from a grange hall. Approx. 6′ H × 40" W × 24" D
Photo courtesy Helga Photo Studio; Private collection

Wall Painting

While there are few wall paintings available in the marketplace, there are a number of murals or wall paintings installed in period museum settings, often taken from their original homes. There are also many still extant in New England homes and buildings, which were executed in the nineteenth century. Original painted walls are often discovered when layers of older wallpaper or paint are removed. Even though the paintings are usually attached to their original plaster walls, their value can be extraordinarily high because of their rarity. Some significant names include Moses Eaton and Rufus Porter.

Furniture

Noted furniture decorators Include Moses Eaton, John Flory, the Mahantango Alphabet Decorators, Thomas Matteson, Johannes Ranck, Christian Seltzer, and Johannes Spitler.

Footstools

Footstools, also known as "crickets," vary widely in shape and material. Tops are commonly made of wood, woven rush, splint, leather, or fabric. Legs are straight or curved, turned, and varied in height. Sometimes the entire footstool assumed painted animal forms such as frogs and turtles. Animal footstool kits and/or instructions for making these animal footstools were widely distributed in the early part of the twentieth century.

Calligraphic Drawing

Calligraphic drawings are pen and ink sketches of birds, animals, flora, and fauna, which were sometimes colored and included elaborate penmanship. These pictures flourished in the nineteenth century and developed from the teaching of penmanship as a school subject. Ornamental writing became more than a utilitarian skill to meet the demands of commerce, and grew into a modest art form. The concentric curvilinear strokes were called flourishes because they were executed in very rapid succession.

Landscapes/House Portraits

Paintings of town views reached a height of popularity between 1840 and 1880. Folk artists satisfied their clientele with their attention to detail and alteration of perspective to include many vantage points from a single view. It was also common as one became more affluent to commission a painting of one's home, sometimes including even the outbuildings. Some significant artists include Thomas Chambers, Erastus Salisbury Field, Charles Hoffman, Joseph H. Hidley, Jurgan Frederick Huge, Grandma Moses, Eunice Pinney, John Rassmussen, Paul Seifert, and Susan Waters.

Marine Paintings also known as Seascapes and Ship Portraits

From its earliest days, America has had a romance with the sea. Professional and amateur painters painted seascapes and ship portraits alike. A distinctive, naïve

Portrait of a Ship, the Steam Paddle Wheeler MATTANO
Inscribed "Draw & painted by James Bard, NY 162 Perry St NY 1859."
29" H × 48 1/2" W
Provenance: Fendelman Sale, Sotheby's New York, October 1993
Photo courtesy David Wheatcroft Antiques; Private collection

American style of ship portraiture and marine paintings developed among anonymous painters and others like John and James Bard, J. F. Huge, and Thomas Chambers. Marine artists worked in oil, pastel, watercolor, and sandpaper drawings. Other artists are J. O. J. Frost and Antonio Jacobsen.

Ship Models

Ship models are decorative objects often created by seamen using simple tools: a jackknife, awl, needle, and file. The most collectible examples are the fully rigged models of actual ships. Eclectic folk art forms include composite features of no specific ship, but several vessels, and are frequently named after a daughter, wife, or sweetheart. Ambitious artisans created dioramas (three-dimensional scenes) in which a fully rigged ship or half model was placed against a background simulating an ocean setting.

Shop and Cigar Store Figures

The cigar store figure was most popular during the last half of the nineteenth century. Makers of cigar store figures tended to include artisans who had been forced to find new ways of income when the market for figureheads and other ship carvings declined. Not all cigar figures were Indians. Many were popular figures such as

foreigners (Turks), average folk (preachers, ladies of fashion, policemen, sailors), characters of folklore and history (Punch, Sir Walter Raleigh), American symbols (Uncle Sam), and topical notables (Dolly Yarden, Admiral Dewey). By the early 1900s, sidewalk obstruction laws prohibited these figures from being set in front of shops, and what has been called the most popular trade sign ever known became all but extinct by 1925. Some known makers of cigar store figures are John Cromwell, Julius T. Melchers, and Samuel Robb.

Portraits

Arising from English and Dutch traditions during the first half of the nineteenth century, itinerant, untutored American limners profited from a rising middle class seeking to display their status in portraits. Media used included oil, pastel, and watercolor. The paintings are now appreciated as social historical documents as well as art. Some noted artists are Ruth Henshaw Bascom, Zedekiah Belknap, John Blunt, John Bradley, John Brew-

The "Eliab Eaton and Lucretia Flint" Family Tree and Memorial

c. Circa 1835, New England, probably executed by Sarah B. Eaton.

Watercolor and ink on paper in the original paint decorated architectural frame including a combination of both a family tree noting the births of the Eaton's twelve children and a memorial noting the deaths of some family members, with three inset poems along the bottom section and a scrolled pediment with an inset oval mirror along the top. 23 1/4" H × 25 3/4" W framed. Photo courtesy Frank & Barbara Pollack American Antiques & Art

ster, Jr., Winthrop Chandler, Joseph H. Davis, Emily Eastman, James Sanford Ellsworth, Erastus Salisbury Field, Jonathan Fisher, Deborah Goldsmith, Sturtevant Hamblin, Rufus Hathaway, William Jennys, Joshua Johnson, Jacob Maentel, Reuben Moulthrop, Noah North, Sheldon Peck, Elizabeth Perkins, the Beardsley Limner, Ammi Phillips, Rufus Porter, Asahel Powers, William Matthew Prior, the Reading Artist, Samuel A. and Ruth W. Shute, Joseph Whiting Stock, Gus Wilson, and Maryann Willson.

Pastel or Pencil Drawings on Paper

Names of note in this medium are Ferdinand Brader, Fritz Vogt, and Micah Williams.

Shaker Spiritual or Inspirational Drawings

Inspirational drawings and paintings produced between the 1840s and 1850s reflect the Shaker religious love for nature and their tendency to see the world in a strict and orderly fashion. Symbols are placed in the art to tell a specific story. Trees, flowers, and fruit are often used and have various meanings. Few of these drawings are in private hands so when they appear at auction their prices reflect their rarity.

History Paintings

Historical paintings tell the story of life in nineteenth-century America. These works of art could also serve as records of family events, another important means of understanding life in our forebears' times. Edward Hicks and Horace Pippin are recognized names in this genre.

Religious/Fantasy Paintings

Artists of note are Ralph & Martha Cahoon, Erastus Salisbury Field, Edward Hicks, Morris Hirschfield, and Horace Pippin.

Ethnic/Religious Art

Rooted in a medieval style of lettering, frakturs (literally meaning "broken writings") were stylized, decorative watercolor pictures painted by hand or mass-produced by printing. German-Americans created them between 1750 and 1850 to record important events and depict spiritual subjects. Among the wide range of fraktur were birth, baptismal, and wedding certificates, house blessings, family registers, and rewards of merit. The heart, tulip, and distelfink were popular motifs. The highest prices are paid for handcrafted fraktur by identified artists. Well-known names are Samuel Bentz, the Mount Pleasant Artist, the Ephrata Cloister, the Cross-Legged Angel Artist, David Culp, Johann Adam Eyer, Susannah Heebner, Frederick Otto Krebs, Rudolph Landes, Christian Mertel, Daniel Otto, Heinrich Otto, Francis Portzline, Durs Rudy, Johannes Ernst Spangenberg, Jacob Strickler, the Sussel-Washington Artist, John Van Minian, and Henry Young.

Silhouettes

Profile paper cuttings, or shades, are usually cut black negatives depicting a head-and-shoulder portrait against a white ground, although reverse procedures are known as well. The term derived from the eighteenth-century profile portraitist and finance minister Etienne de Silhouette, and they were popular in America from 1790 to 1850, when they yielded to the daguerreotype.

Visionary
Names to look for are William Edmondson, Elijah Pierce, and Edgar Tolson.

Sculpture
Toys
Rocking horses were a favorite toy among young American children during the nineteenth century. Many examples have survived and show wide gradations of skill among the craftsmen. They range from the very primitive woodcarvings to the elaborate full-figured horse with leather ears and real horsehair tails. Noah's ark was another popular toy. The many hand-carved miniature wooden animals provided hours of entertainment and enjoyment for American children. The variety of animal breeds enabled one to learn these different species.

Architectural Elements
These include buildings, marine and furniture. Names of note are James Hampton and John Scholl.

Ship carving
This area includes figureheads as well as decorative sculptural objects. One of the most significant carvers is John Haley Bellamy.

Tramp Art
Tramp Art is layered cigar, fruit, or vegetable boxes decorated with notched chip or edge carving and then fashioned into boxes, frames, pieces of furniture, and sculpture. This craft form was prevalent from the 1880s through the 1930s when cigar boxes were commonly given or thrown away after the cigars were smoked.

Baskets
Baskets served many utilitarian purposes in American life, both in the home and on the farm. Baskets were commonly made from found materials such as split woods (ash, hickory, or oak), sweet grasses, willow rods, or wicker. Shapes included ovals, rectangles, rounds, or squares with center or side handles depending upon need. Purposes ranged from gathering, storing, and transporting foods and light objects to trapping eels.

Potato stamped baskets using vegetable dyes, usually made and decorated by Native Americans in the northeastern part of the United States are highly prized by collectors, especially those with dates or initials on them. Other types of these containers include Nantucket, Pennsylvania German, and Shaker baskets.

Ceramics
Chalkware

Popularly made in Pennsylvania, and consisting of processed gypsum or plaster of Paris and water, chalkware was factory cast in molds into fashion ornaments resembling more expensive pottery and porcelain figures. The white plaster of Paris, hollow-bodied objects, commercially produced in quantity between 1850 and 1890, were sized and hand painted in both oil and watercolor. Brightly colored, the unglazed images often depicted animals and birds (cats, rooster, sheep, parrots), fruit forms, busts of famous people, and churches.

Redware

Redware pottery is made from red or brown clay thrown on a potter's wheel and fired at a low temperature. It was manufactured throughout the United States into the nineteenth century. The clay occurs naturally and requires simple kilns to make. Utilitarian shapes were limited to basic functional forms such as plates, bowls, and jars. Variety was most often evident in the slip or clay-

Tramp Art Bank
Early twentieth century, unusual steel bank with tramp art chipped carving and brass tack accents.
6" H × 6" W
Private collection

Paint Decorated Pine Wall Cupboard
c. Mid-eighteenth century. New England
With molded cornice above an arched upper
section with two shaped shelves, over a single
lower door, supported by cutout feet, retains old
red painted surface. 8" H × 28 1/2" W

Stoneware Crock with Lid, Late nineteenth
century, Pennsylvania. With overall cobalt floral
decoration. 6" H

**Redware Flower Pot with Attached Under
Tray,** Late nineteenth century. Shenandoah
Valley, Virginia. With green and brown glaze
over a cream ground. 8" H, 7 1/2" Dia.

Redware Egg Cup, Late nineteenth century,
Possibly Bell Pottery, Shenandoah Valley,
Virginia. With green and orange manganese
decoration. 2 1/2" H

Stoneware Crock with Lid, Late nineteenth
century, Pennsylvania. With overall tulip
decoration. 7" H

Two-Gallon Stoneware Jug, Late nineteenth
century, Pennsylvania. Impressed "D.P.
Shenfelder Reading, PA, 2" With stylized cobalt
floral decoration. 14" H

One-Piece Walnut Corner Cupboard, Mid-
eighteenth century, Pennsylvania. Top and
bottom doors with wrought iron rattail hinges,
resting on a flat base; with some restorations.
55" H × 27" W Provenance: Southampton
Historical Museum (NY); Ex collection: Henry
Francis du Pont

Three-Gallon Stoneware Crock, Late
nineteenth century, New York. Impressed "W.
Roberts Binghampton, NY." With cobalt bird on
branch decoration. 12" H

Three-Gallon Stoneware Water Cooler, Late
nineteenth century, Pennsylvania. With double-
sided cobalt floral decoration. 15" H. Photo
courtesy Pook & Pook

trailed designs (usually yellow) or in the brushed splotches of other colorants such as manganese. Plates with names or unusual colors, such as green or blue, are rare and highly prized by collectors. The names to look for are John Bell, George Huebner, John Leidy, the Medinger Family, Conrad Mumbauer, John Solliday, and David Spinner.

Stoneware

Stoneware is durable, hard pottery made from a blend of high-fired clays. Since the clay was found in relatively few locations, and the firing had to be done in kilns able to withstand high temperatures, the manufacture of stoneware was restricted to central areas. Ease of transport was also crucial, both for the import of materials and the export of finished wares. Stoneware potteries flourished during the nineteenth century. The most common forms of stoneware were crocks, jugs, and churns. Their shapes were regionally quite uniform but differed in surface design. Much early stoneware has incised decoration. In the nineteenth century, northern centers in Bennington, Vermont, New York, New Jersey, and Pennsylvania created elaborate slip trailed and brushed designs of birds, flowers, and animals in cobalt blue. Many potteries in Ohio, Pennsylvania, and West Virginia used stencil decoration. Southern potteries often glazed their pots in dark earthen tones. Significant names in stoneware are Anna Pottery, the Crolius Family, E. and L. Norton, John Remmey, "Bennington" pottery/Rockingham glaze, Edgefield wares, and Face Jugs.

Commercial Sculpture—Including Advertising, Barter and Carnival
Advertising

Prior to Noah Webster's standardization of American English in 1825, uniform public literacy was inconsistent in the United States. Signs identified shops and services, the local tavern/inn's location, charges for roads, bridges, and ferry crossings, and travel directions. Two-dimensional painted signs displayed animals, birds, and fanciful abstractions. Three-dimensional carved figures included Gabriel calling the townsfolk to drink, barber poles, boots for boot makers, teeth for dentists, fish for fish markets,

and eyeglasses for opticians. It was common for portrait, coach, and house painters to also paint trade signs.

Barter
Well-known names of wood carvers are Clark Coe, Aaron Mountz, John Reber, and Wilhelm Schimmel.

Carousel Figures
Carousel figures, crafted in a dozen or more northern East Coast shops, were popular from 1875–1925. Amusement park and country fair carousels primarily sported carved and painted wooden horses and menagerie animals. Though some were relief carvings, the majority were carved in the round. Highly treasured for their sculptural quality, condition, original paint, and structural soundness, it appears that tasteful, skillful restoration does not significantly lessen an animal's value. Names of note are Dentzel, Herschel-Spillman, Charles Loof, Illions, Stein, and Goldstein, and the Philadelphia Toboggan Company.

Dolls
Cloth and rag dolls, among the most popular type of dolls, were the simplest to make. Scrap material and some stuffing—straw or cotton—sufficed. Cloth doll features were either painted or embroidered and the hair was made from threads, yarn, or animal or human hair.

It was also common for a father, uncle, or brother to carve a piece of wood into a facsimile for the child, boy or girl, in the family. Frequently painted and/or clothed as the recipient desired, dolls considered to be folk art are one of a kind. Included within this category are hand-made marionettes and other carved wooden figures such as balancing and jump toys.

Metalware
Iron
Cast- and wrought iron figures were among the most ubiquitous types of objects found during the last half of the nineteenth century. The images were molded and hence were produced in multiples, though their paint often personalized them. Among the kinds of objects that today's collectors seek are shooting gallery targets, doorstops, nutcrackers, boot scrapers and bootjacks, mill weights, hitching post finials, andirons, kitchen utensils, irons, flower holders, and various molds used for food. Since many pieces functioned both outdoors and indoors and were subject to much use, it is very rare to find old cast- or wrought-iron forms that are not weathered or worn (pitted). Peter Derr was a well-known ironmonger. Other names of note are D. Gilbert, John Shade, and Willoughby Shade.

Tinware
Tin was a popular material for teapots, candle sconces, chandeliers, and document boxes. Kitchen utensils were also fashioned from this durable metal. It was common to decorate tinware by painting it. Tinware is sometimes mistakenly called toleware. Toleware is actually classically ornamented French-painted tinware. Another means of decorating tin is to dent the surface with a hammer and nail. When holes are created, the result is called pierced tin. Some important decorators of paint-decorated tinware are Ann Butler, Sarah Upson, and Amelia Filley.

Religious Art
Traditionally there has been marketplace resistance to owning religious art. There are exceptions to this statement especially in the areas of Shaker art, Amish quilts and Southwestern woodcarvings.

Gravestones

Colonial New England gravestones were carved in tradi-tional motifs including angels, willow trees, and geomet-ric symbols. Most often produced by professional stonecutters and carvers, these carvings were one of the first American-made sculptures.

Santos

A great deal of southwestern American religious folk art derives from Roman Catholicism and is in origin. Most pieces were made from soft, porous wood such as pon-derosa pine that was covered with gesso and applied paint would adhere more easily.

Scherenschnitte

Scherenschnitte are paper cuttings derived from central European traditions. The earliest American forms are from the late eighteenth century and were love letters (liebesbrief) and birth certificates (taufschein). Various Protestant sects such as the Moravians, Seventh Day Baptists of Ephrata, Scwenkfelders, Mennonites, and many adherents of the Lutheran and Reformed churches produced this type of work. Scherenschnitte uses a tech-nique of cutting paper in a continuous design after fold-

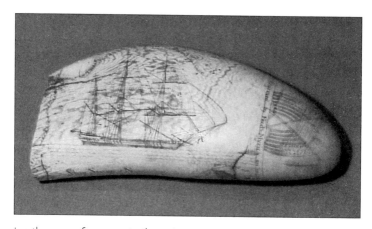

ing the paper from one to three times for uniform pattern repeats, and it should not be confused with paper cuttings made by using a knife.

Scrimshaw

Scrimshaw signifies incised or engraved carvings on whalebone and whale teeth executed primarily by sailors associated with the American whaling industry during the nineteenth century. Simple jackknives, sail needles, files, and saws made from barrel hoops functioned as tools. After being carved and etched, the design was highlighted by rubbing it with a mixture of a varnish fixative and ink. This darkened the carved design on the ivory. In addition to such utilitarian items as bodkins, boxes, busks, canes, clothespins, dippers, ditty boxes, jagging wheels, pie crimpers, plaques, rolling pins, yarn winders, and swifts, scrimshaw or scrimshaw decoration appears on whimsies and whale's teeth themselves. Frederick Myrick and Susan's teeth are important names in this area of collecting.

Tavern and Trade Signs

These items date back to a time when only a limited part of the population could read. Due to this, those with shops or trades needed to advertise their wares in a graphic manner. Signage was an important means of luring customers into one's establishment.

Wood Carvings

Carvers, sometimes called whittlers, like Wilhelm Schimmel of Pennsylvania, created small figures, toys, and other decorative objects for their own or other's enjoyment. Eagles, cats, owls, and roosters were popular figures, as well as human forms frequently depicting caricatures, notable personages, and spiritual entities. The humor often imbued into the pieces makes them endearing for folk art aficionados.

Bird and Fishing Decoys

Originally used by the Native Americans, bird decoys reached the height of their popularity in the late nineteenth century and early twentieth centuries. There are distinct regional characteristics that make identification possible. Categorically, decoys are waterfowl (floater) and shore bids (stick-ups). Floaters such as mallards, pintails, canvasbacks, mergansers, scooters, and eiders ride the waters of bays, marshes, lakes, inlets, and oceans. Shore birds, i.e., sandpipers, yellowlegs, curlews, and pipers, are mounted on sticks set into the ground. Another important decoy category includes those not hunted for food. Crows were hunted as pests or for sport. Owls were used to bait their natural enemy, the crow. Gulls and swans were used as confidence decoys signaling safety and food to other birds. Fish decoy making reached its height during the 1830s. Unlike bird decoys, they do not have to represent specific species to be effective. As a result, fish decoys are often painted in a whimsical fashion. Made with an appropriate lead weight inset underneath, their length can vary from 3 to 48 inches. Pine was favored because it carves and floats easily. Individualistic carving often identifies age, region, and maker. Other forms of decoys include frogs, turtles, muskrats, and mice. Plastic, rubber, and metal versions notwithstanding, most fish decoys are handmade. Important makers include A. Elmer Crowell, John Dilley, and Joe Lincoln, those made by Native Americans, Oscar Peterson and Lem & Steve Ward.

Canes/Walking Sticks

Walking sticks or canes are practical, fashionable wooden items which were primarily made from 1850 to 1900, typically created from sturdy domestic hickory, ash, spruce, or imported mahogany. Country craftsmen

and amateurs personalized canes with paint, root handles, carved figures, incised decoration, bone, and/or ivory. Canes were especially popular in the southern part of the United States. Most cane makers, like so many American folk artists, are unknown. One name to look for is "Schtockschnitzler" Simmons.

Weathervanes

Weathervanes were used to forecast weather conditions. The first symbols were sheet iron or wooden banners and religious figures depicting the cockerel and angel Gabriel. Until the mid-nineteenth century, virtually all weathervanes were handcrafted. With the arrival of the Industrial Age, however, notable commercial vane makers like J. W. Fiske of New York City and J. Harris & Son of Boston, Massachusetts, were established. Companies like these began to use molds to form full-figured animals, people, and other familiar images. The eagle became a favorite design motif, as did patriotic figures such as George Washington, Columbia, and figures of Liberty. Animals such as pigs, horses, and cows appeared as well. Names to know are L. W. Cushing, Cushing & White, Shem Drowne, J. W. Fiske, J. Harris & Son, Howard & Co., A. L. Jewell, J. L. Mott, W. A. Snow and the Rochester Iron Works.

Shorebird Glass-Eyed Plover Decoy Early twentieth century, eastern United States. Hand carved and paint decorated wood. 12" L Private collection

Rooster Weathervane
c.1880, L. W. Cushing & Sons, Waltham, Mass. Full-bodied copper weathervane with unusual split tail and two copper balls below. Approximately 34" H
Photo courtesy David Wheatcroft Antiques

Whirligigs

Also called wind toys, whirligigs were fashioned from wood and/or metal by untrained artists. These carvings, in either silhouette or three-dimensional form, were constructed with either paddle-like arms (baffles) or multi-figured objects with propellers that catch the wind and turn the crank. Whirligigs often satirized animals or people, making social statements through their motion's rate of speed. Their forerunner may well have been the scarecrow.

Textiles
Coverlets

Woven coverlets are bed coverings usually made of wool and cotton and include overshot, summer/winter, double-weave, Jacquard, and Biederwand types. These geometric and curvilinear bedcovers were useful and popular in the eighteen and nineteenth centuries. Professional itinerant male weavers traveled from town to

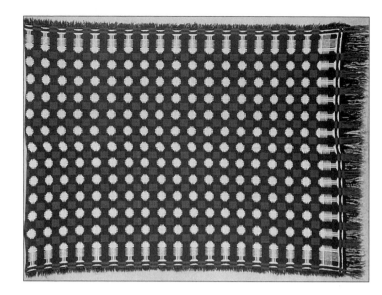

town with their looms seeking orders during the mid- and late nineteenth century. Types of coverlets include double-woven, Jacquard and overshot.

Two-Panel Hand-Woven Coverlet Early nineteenth century, New England. Approximately 73" H × 82" L Private collection

Quilts

A quilt is a bed covering consisting of three layers: a top, filling, and back. The layers are joined by either tying or stitching the layers together. Types of quilts include whole cloth, pieced, and appliquéd, or a combination of these types. Quilt patterns are often abstract and in geometrical forms, but patterns might also be naturalistic. There are many quilt names such as Album, Friendship, Patriotic, and Log Cabin. Outstanding regional examples are noted among Baltimore Album quilts and the vividly graphic examples made by the Amish and Mennonite sects. Names to be familiar with include Amish, appliqué, broderie perse, crazy quilts, linsey-woolsey, and pieced quilts.

Rugs (for table and bed)

Hooked rugs became popular at the end of the nineteenth century. Primitive designs were executed as fabric-dyed strips of wool were worked into a backing material with a special hook. Geometric patterns as well as flowers, animals, and houses were favored designs. Two dis-

Family Record Sampler
c. 1835, Pennington, New Jersey, by EureAnn Titus. A grapevine border is characteristic of samplers from the Pennington and Titusville area, south of Trenton. Approximately 18" H × 20" W Photo courtesy M. Finkel & Daughter

tinct, identifiable hooked rug styles may be noted. From the Grenfell Handicrafts cooperative in Newfoundland and Labrador come some fine hooked mats. During the middle of the nineteenth century, Edward Frost, from Maine, introduced pre-stamped rug designs on burlap. The Frost pre-printed patterns popularized and spread the craft. Braided rugs first appeared in the early nineteenth century and are technically one of the simplest types of rugs to execute. After braiding strips of cut fabric, the fabric pieces are usually sewn into circular or oval shapes. Color patterning was usually random but the Shakers created some exceptional color-controlled examples. In the hooked rug area Edward Sand Frost and Dr. William Grenfell are names to recognize. Shirred, yarn sewn, and Waldoboro are styles of rugs.

Mourning Pictures

Mourning or memorial pictures were a European tradition that immigrated to the United States late in the eighteenth century. Created primarily by young girls at

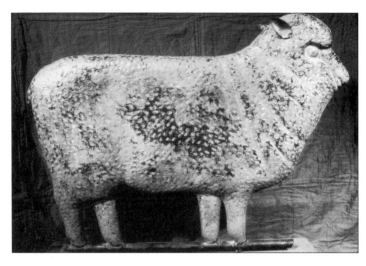

Ram Weathervane
Late nineteenth century, L. W. Cushing & Sons, Waltham, Massachusetts. Hand-hammered copper with gilt finish, well-executed and full-bodied design. 36" H Private collection

Deer Weathervane
Late nineteenth century, New England. Hand-hammered copper with gilt finish, well-executed and full-bodied design. 36" H × 24" L Private collection

finishing schools or academies, this art could include watercolor on paper, needlework or pieces of jewelry. Predominant symbols like the weeping willow tree, tombstones, and other symbols of death were often depicted in these pictures.

Ram Weathervane, Late nineteeneth century, Attributed to L. W. Cushing & Sons, Waltham, Massachusetts. Molded and gilded copper with gilt and verdigris finish, with modeled fleece and curled sheet copper horns. 31" H × 36" L Private collection.

Theorem, c. Mid-nineteenth century, New England. Oil on velvet depicting a bowl of fruit with cherries and grapes, with some foxing. Approximately 24" × 36" Photo courtesy Helga Photo Studio; Private collection

Samplers and Needlework Pictures Including Seminary Work

Samplers are ornamental needlework examples, which often include a variety of embroidered stitches and may indicate the maker's name, dates, alphabets, numerals, designs, and pictorial elements. Types of samplers include band, alphabet, verse, pictorial family record, map, and a combination of all of these types. Originating from a long European and Continental tradition, early American samplers were reference pieces used to learn to mark precious household textiles. During the last quarter

Theorem,
Dated 1867,
New England.
Watercolor on
paper of a glass
compote of fruit
on a smoke
decorated
tabletop.
Approximately
14" H × 17" W
Private
collection

Theorem,
c. Mid-
nineteenth
century, New
England.
Watercolor on
paper of a vase
filled with
flowers.
Approximately
36" H × 24" W
Photo courtesy
Helga Photo
Studio; Private
collection

Trotting Horse Hooked Rug, Early twentieth century, New England. Multicolored fabric hooked rug with a horse in the center surrounded by a zigzag border. Approximately 24" H × 36" W Photo courtesy Victor Weinblatt

Jumping Horse Hooked Rug, Mid-nineteenth century, Upper New York State. Multicolored fabric hooked rug with a horse jumping a fence in the center surrounded by stars, hearts, and geometrics. 34 1/2" H × 66" W Photo courtesy Betty Sterling, Brainstorm Farm Antiques

Horse with Chicken Bone Hooked Rug
Late nineteenth century, American.
Multicolored fabric hooked rug with a horse
surrounded by two small dogs, a heart, stars, a
pair of shoes and clover leaf devices; the
symbolic meaning of what looks like a chicken
bone in the center of the horse is unknown.
Approximately 37" H × 44" W
Private collection

of the eighteenth and the first quarter of the nineteenth centuries, sampler making functioned as an essential "accomplishment" in the female academic curriculum. Regional styles developed; the best known include the Mary Balch School in Providence, Rhode Island, and the Westtown School in Westtown, Pennsylvania, among others. Fully realized pictorial samplers, otherwise known as needlework pictures, were embroidered genre, mythological or fantasy scenes loosely based upon prints.

Pin Pricked Pictures
Most often combined with watercolor or pen, pencil, or pastel drawings, pinpricking was another way to decorate an image. This European tradition, was most popular in the United States at the turn of the nineteenth century, and was literally made using a pin to make holes in the picture to emphasize its look. The decorative pinpricks could also form the image.

Outsider Art
Names of note are Eddie Arning, Miles Carpenter, William Edmondson, Minnie Evans, Ralph Fasanella, William Hawkins, John Kane, Sister Gertrude Morgan,

Portrait of a Young Woman
Mid-nineteenth century, New England, by William Matthew Prior.
Oil on academy board. 14" H × 9 13/16" W
Private collection

Portrait of a Young Woman
Mid-nineteenth century, New England, by William Matthew Prior.
Oil on academy board. 14" H × 9 13/16" W
Private collection

Elijah Pierce, Martin Ramirez, Judith Scott, Jimmy Lee Sudduth, Bill Traylor, and Adolf Wolfli.

What Is It? An Image of Object Tutorial

The illustrations accompanying this book are here to provide an image database for you to start to learn what the objects look like and how to look at them. Now that you are familiar with the names of some of the makers and what some of the categories of American folk art are, there is no substitute for the objects themselves! In some instances, the image shown may be by a listed maker; in many cases they will not. Again, most makers of American folk art are no longer known, and many of the objects themselves are now obsolete for their original purpose.

With objects illustrated, we have included four different examples to underscore the idea of "good, better, and best." The fact that "good" represents the baseline acceptability for a work of American folk art should not be taken in any way as a criticism of the object or the standard —"good" American folk art is hard to find. "Better" and "best" are those objects in which either one detail— a motif, a color, a signature, or even the subject—for ex-

ample—or the relative quality of its manufacture places the object on an ascending scale of desirability.

In the illustration for portraiture, three works attributable to William Matthew Prior and his Boston atelier are shown. The "good" example is just that—a typical subject (a woman) painted in a typical medium (oil on board) displaying the quintessential brushwork and styling that Prior and his colleagues employed. The painting is a textbook example of the artist's work. The "better" example is the same as the good example, so the only difference is subjective—the sitter is slightly more attractive. The distinction between the two works goes to the heart of what is often difficult about American folk art: Qualitative judgments about works of art are often subjective. The "best" example, a pair of portraits of a little boy and girl, is just like the first two—same medium, same styling—the difference is the desirability of the sitters. In collecting American folk portraits, a general truth is that children are more desirable than adults; couples are more desirable than singles; and women, especially young ones, are more desirable than men. ◨

Portraits of Children
Mid-nineteenth century, New England, by William Matthew Prior. Oil on academy board. Each 14" H × 9¹³/₁₆" W Photo courtesy Sotheby's; Private collection

3

AMERICAN ANTECEDENTS: EUROPEAN FOLK ART

For nearly every example of American folk art there is a European counterpart. In some instances, one almost can't tell the difference between European and American folk art; this is especially true if all other information, such as a history of ownership, has been lost.

Just as the furniture of America's founding colonies is rooted in the European traditions that immigrants

[3] The authors would like to thank Peter S. Seibert, Director of the Heritage Center Museum of Lancaster County in Lancaster, PA, for his assistance with this chapter.

brought to this country, the same is so with American folk art. As English vernacular ways transplanted to New England in particular and its other principal colonies, Dutch traditions settled in New York, the Hudson River Valley, and the Chesapeake; the Protestant Diaspora inspired by the revocation of the Edict of Nantes (1685) coupled with the New World's identity as a land of religious freedom made America a magnet for these refugees. Add to this the African nations whose citizens were brought to America against their will. All of these people brought with them the only thing they could: their cultural heritage. This rich brew of folkways includes not just the surviving material artifacts we call American folk art but other traditions such as social, linguistic, and musical customs and cuisine. In so melding, like a fine dish whose subtle individual flavors enhance the whole, American folk traditions were born. While the specific circumstances of America's early appeal changed over time, political events and religious persecution in other countries continued (and continue) to provide America with a constant and fresh influx of non-native traditions to enrich what is already here.

In discussing the immigrant experience as it relates to the appearance and fabrication of American folk art, it is important to distinguish between "survival" and "revival."

By survival, we mean those traditions and work habits that emigrated unconsciously from country of origin to the new country with the individual artisan and were then taught to the next generation. An example of survival is the tradition of inlaid or paint-decorated blanket chests brought to America by German immigrants in the late seventeenth and eighteenth centuries: Original European forms arrived with their immigrant owners and their production instantly began in America.

By revival, we mean the conscious choice of artisans to adopt a mode of fabrication that is otherwise not within their common and practical experience. An example of revival in America is rosemaling. Rosemaling, the Scandinavian style of carved and/or painted floral decoration (seen on furniture, architecture, and even treen or wooden ware), went out of fashion in its native areas during the mid-nineteenth century. The tradition finds its roots predominantly in Norway, especially the Telemark and Hallingdal valleys, where it was an outgrowth of larger aesthetic shifts toward more classically-based European styles. Like Pennsylvania German paint-decorated furnishings, in which certain styles and motifs are distinct to specific counties, Norwegian rosemaling is regionally distinct as well.

The style was revived in the United States in the twentieth century during the Depression. Per Lysne, a Norwegian native who learned rosemaling in Norway, is generally credited with inspiring the revival in America; he returned to the art form when his business as a coach and sign painter lagged in the early 1930s. Interest in Lysne's work and early artifacts brought to America by their ancestors inspired Scandinavian-Americans in the early twentieth century to take up rosemaling as well. Mirroring Scandinavian immigrant settlement patterns, the revived art has become especially popular in the northern Midwest; it did not, however, take root immediately on arrival as paint-decorated chests did in German-American communities.

Among the nations other than England to lose population to America in the eighteenth century were France, Holland, Switzerland, and the nation-states that now comprise Germany.

Urban centers such as Boston, New York, and Philadelphia, as well as America's South were fertile breeding grounds for these divergent groups. By definition, so-called "Pennsylvania German" folk art (henceforth called 'German-American') is West-Central European and generally Palatinate in origin and is one of the few immigrant cultures to survive today as a distinctly recognizable and historical tradition. (The others include the Spanish Southwest and French Mississippi corridor from Louisiana to Quebec. Each group, German, Spanish, and French, retains a language that both sets it apart from the surrounding countryside yet diverges from its European original. The folk art of each group is also strongly identified with religion in a way that was not the case elsewhere.) German immigrants to America took those traditions much farther, however, than just to Pennsylvania—west to Indiana and south down the Shenandoah Valley to Virginia, West Virginia, and Texas, the Moravian communities of North Carolina, and the more urban locale of Charleston, South Carolina.

The surviving American folk art of these German-American communities presents one of the clearest pictures in which the favored decorative motifs (and in some instances, palette) of a specific immigrant group translate neatly across media—from fraktur to paint-decorated furniture, from quilts to other decorated textiles (samplers, embroidered hand towels), a uniform vocabulary exists. Yet the watercolor portraiture of Jacob Maentel, a German immigrant to Pennsylvania in the early nineteenth century, shows a German community otherwise striving for English homogeneity in its outward appearance. Like New England, where the architecture and vernacular furniture can often be traced back to the region of England from whence those specific colonists came, some German-American fraktur suggest regionalism that may relate to the artist's origin as well. Whereas the majority of German-American fraktur employs a bold graphic palette and style, a small group of German-American fraktur is more delicate, floral, and detailed in its style and uses a softer palette as well.

These works may relate to the type of illuminated manuscript work done in Alsace-Lorraine, an area on the border of France and what is now Germany that changed possession by each of its neighbors several times during the eighteenth and nineteenth centuries. The original Alsatian work, however, tends to include what the American work does not: specifically Catholic imagery including flaming hearts, crowns, cruciforms, and Christian heraldic animals. This religious inclusion presents a certain irony in European versus American fraktur. In Europe, frakturs were done primarily as legal documents and, with the exception of Alsatian examples, were not religious in nature. In America, fraktur assumed a religious and usually German Protestant significance in several of their most prolific forms—baptismal certificates (Taufschein), house blessings (Haus Segen) and writing samples (Vorschriften), all of which often included scriptural texts beyond the inherent religious intent of the first two.

Similarly, whereas France and Holland's Huguenot population settled along the Atlantic coast from Florida and the Carolinas and north to Boston and New York, bringing highly sophisticated designs seen in furniture and silver, this same group also brought more vernacular traditions expressed in less grand forms as well. An early eighteenth-century turned and joined chair with a history of ownership in a coastal South Carolina family came to auction in October 1998 at Christie's New York. The robustly turned form related directly to similar Continental examples in its repeated "sausage" motifs and configuration of structural elements. As scholarship on the chair observed, one-third of the joiners documented in seventeenth-century South Carolina were Huguenot, and by 1700 approximately 325 were of French origin.[4]

The areas of American folk art production that experience the greatest crossover with European examples include decorated furniture (carved, painted, or inlaid), needlework, portraiture, and pottery. Interestingly, some European folk traditions, such as kurbitz painting (a type of impermanent tapestry-on-paper wall decoration usually depicting Biblical scenes that is hung like a frieze and associated with Scandinavian folk art), did not make it to America. Others, as discussed with rosemaling, came much later. Similarities also exist between such forms as decoys and carousel figures. Yet, where the marketplace is concerned, these latter two forms are simultaneous enough in Europe and America that there may not be an issue of aesthetic roots or transplanting to discuss. Like many examples of European and American folk art, once an object's specific identity is lost, it is almost impossible to distinguish one from another.

Paint-Decorated Furniture

America's paint-decorated furniture traditions drew from several different sources and remained essentially unique to their transplanted region in the New World. Whether antique American paint-decorated furniture is

[4] Jennifer Olshin, *Important American Furniture and Decorative Arts*, Christie's New York, October 8, 1998, lot 36, pp.30–33.

discussed in terms of American folk art, or whether it is discussed in the more highbrow academic terms of vernacular furniture traditions, generally depends upon who is leading the discussion and the specific genre of material. Fancier auction houses tend to distinguish the two according to value: Paint-decorated furniture that brings little money is American folk art; paint-decorated furniture that brings high prices belongs to a "vernacular furniture tradition." The same is true of paintings—higher-priced works are often scavenged by more glamorous "American Painting" departments; lower-priced works become American folk art. These are opportunistic marketing ploys rather than real appreciation of the work. Whether presented in terms of folk or furniture, antique American paint-decorated furniture is, in fact, all the same and needs to be considered as a whole.

The principal European sources for American paint-decorated furniture are England, Holland, the Germanic states of central Europe, and Switzerland. England's paint-decorated furniture appeared in that country's primary area of settlement in New England, most notably western Massachusetts and the Connecticut River Valley, where forms such as sunflower type and Hadley chests were both originally brightly paint-decorated and carved, a very distinct tradition from rosemaling. Hadley chests were made in the latter part of the seventeenth and early part of the eighteenth century in the Hadley, Massachusetts, area and are distinguished by their exuberant floral carving. The grisaille paint-decorated tradition of Holland, in which furniture was painted in imitation of carved stone, transplanted to the Dutch communities of the Hudson River Valley of New York. As discussed at length earlier, a variety of paint decorating traditions emigrated from West Central Europe and Switzerland straight to the Germanic settlements of the Mid-Atlantic and the South. Additional modes of decorating furniture, such as inlay and carving, were also brought to this country from France (Canadian and Mississippi Valley furniture) and Spain (Florida and the American Southwest).

Needlework
Needlework proficiency was a function of women's education in both England and America, and England is the

primary aesthetic source for American needlework. With educational mores in the two countries essentially mirroring each other, it is often difficult to distinguish between the two. This is true particularly where earlier tent-stitched, stump work, or Charles II–type needlework is concerned. This is also evident in needlework in which the school has not yet been identified, and otherwise distinguishing features are indeterminate as well. The simplicity and layout of English Quaker needlework translates, but is not identical, to Quaker needlework in the Philadelphia area and surrounding communities.

Portraiture

In addition to needlework, portraiture may also be the single largest area of American artistic production in which England and its divergent portrait traditions informed and related to the appearance of similar works in America. Two principal traditions emigrated from England and evolved in America, one being more important to American folk art than the other: the Anglo-Dutch style of portraiture, in which a subject might be portrayed with heraldic devices, or an 'AE' indicating the sitter's age, and identifying symbols of power, wealth, trade or accomplishments in a two-dimensional and static manner, is usually in a dark palette, lacking a specific light source or vantage point. This older English portrait tradition informed seventeenth-century New England portraiture, and is the ground in which the American folk limner tradition took its roots. Another is a post-Renaissance, courtlier style of portraiture, promulgated by London's Royal Academy of Art, informed that group of American trained professional artists, such as Benjamin West, John Singleton Copley, and Gilbert Stuart. This international style of portraiture, seen in its day as the more accomplished and sophisticated of the two, is the type that was preferred by America's urban elite and was used, for example, for state portraits of George Washington. A tradition of itinerant portraiture exists as much in England as it did in the United States. Again, in cases where an English folk portrait might have been brought to the United States, and lacking any other information, there is little chance of differentiating it from an American example. Other European portrait traditions existed in America as well, though to a vastly lesser degree than those from England. The influences of Spain and France are seen in some itinerant portraits from Florida and the Gulf of Mexico region.

Pottery

Pottery represents one of the most interesting international and temporal intersections of decorative arts. England made redware pottery similar to that seen in America; slip-decorated redware made at the same time as some American examples are almost identical in appearance and decoration. Some experts argue that the body color differs from one to the other or that the underside color differs. France made redware pottery similar to American pieces. Jaspé ware, French redware made during the second half of the nineteenth century in the Savoie region of France, is also remarkably similar to American slip-decorated redware in form and decoration. Jaspé ware sells in the United States for a fraction of the price of its American counterparts and, therefore, is sometimes collected as an attractive and less expensive alternative to American wares. Swiss and Scandinavian examples of slip-decorated and sgraffito redware pottery have frequently been mistaken for German-American and Moravian redware examples. Most recently, in the 1970s, an entire group of newly made Mexican sprig-decorated (bas-relief appliqués, usually floral) redware pottery was introduced in the marketplace as Pennsylvania and Shenandoah pottery. Although the methods of making and applying decorative motifs are similar, the pottery is not American. The endurance and universality of materials, motifs, and fabrication methods in redware pottery alone underscore the critical importance of examining American folk art not in a vacuum but in an international context.

A few specific areas of American folk art are distinctly American. Likewise, similar to kurbitz painting, a few specific areas of European folk art did not make the voyage to America. Prisoner of War art, carved ivory sculpture generally made by French prisoners during the Napoleonic wars, is related to scrimshaw and ship modeling but is more detailed, smaller in scale, and easily distinguished from its distant American scrimshaw cousin. Regarding English versus American needlework, "woolies," embroidered wool pictures usually showing ship scenes, are generally English, mostly nineteenth-century, and made by sailors to pass the time rather than schoolgirls as part of their studies. Where German-American fraktur is concerned, forms like Vorschriften are unique to America but European Taufpatenbrief (confirmation letters) do not appear in America. Further, Mahantango Valley paint-decorated furniture is generally considered a uniquely American innovation in its union of English case furniture with Germanic decoration. ◩

4

THE HISTORY OF AMERICAN FOLK ART

The history of American folk art is a two-part narrative. There is not only the history of the objects themselves, the disparate people who made them, and changes over time in technology and social customs that affected the appearance and nature of these objects, but there is also the history of the marketplace. An efficient economy created by collectors, dealers, and curators has also come to define what American folk art means. Contemporary folk artists, working in a manner outside the norms of academia and mainstream culture, show that American folk art continues today. These "outsider artists," as they are called in the marketplace, create painting and sculp-

Birth and Baptismal Certificate for Lydia Berckenstock, Born 14 August 1797 to Johan and Fronica Berckenstock

c. 1797, Upper Milford Township, Lehigh County, Pennsylvania, by. Durs Rudy. Watercolor and ink on paper, with central banded heart flanked by angels, garlanded flowers, perched birds of Paradise and two small laurel-framed roundels inscribed with blessings centering an Angel Sofia and flanked by red and yellow buildings on landscape. 7⅝" H × 9⅝" W Photo courtesy David Wheatcroft Antiques

ture in a wholly different tradition from American folk artists of the nineteenth century and earlier.

America's first people, its native population, created the earliest American folk art. In decorating and seeking to make otherwise functional tools beautiful—a lidded basket embellished with porcupine quills, a broad spoon whose carved handle represents a bird's head, an early feather-covered decoy used for duck hunting—Native Americans must be credited with the first production of an American artistic tradition identifiable by nation, much as how later European-American folk art can be defined by region or immigrant group.

Subsequent European immigrant cultures created a variety of furniture, paintings, and functional objects whose decoration links them to their homeland. Today, these forms also comprise what we think of as American folk art. In their own time, these objects were not considered art, but everyday furnishings that served a functional purpose, whether physical or social. The community values reflected in American folk art were as simple as a needlework indicating a young girl's education, readiness for

marriage, and the implied wealth of her family (not only that they could afford seminary tuition but that they could afford not to have their daughter assisting with chores at home). A child's birth and Christian baptism documented in a Pennsylvania German fraktur reveals the importance of this religious ritual to the German-American community. Portraits—status symbols previously reserved for the aristocracy and super-rich of the 1600s and 1700s—became affordable to Americans in the 1800s. The paintings routinely include iconography attesting to the wealth, literacy, piety, employment, property ownership, or other prominence of the sitter. In addition to providing warmth, quilts celebrated friendships, life events and, in some instances, provided a creative

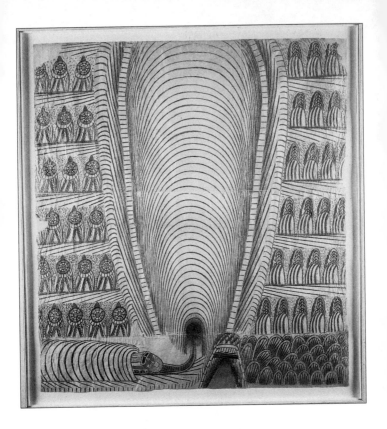

Super Chief,
colored pencil,
ink, crayon,
collage on
paper, 51" × 54,"
c. 1953. Photo
courtesy
Fleisher/Ollman
Gallery

outlet for makers in otherwise strict religious communities, such as the Amish.

Folk art collectors also draw a distinction between those everyday items made by individuals or small shops described above—quilts, furniture, textiles, small decorated tools, etc.—and later nineteenth-century factory-made production items. This latter group, including weathervanes, cigar store figures, trade signs, some decoys (those made by factories), and carousel figures, has come to include a variety of advertising, carnival, and commercial art. Unique examples of these forms made by individuals also exist.

In many ways, interest and the market for Outsider Art is a natural outgrowth of the original mission of early American folk art collectors promoting contemporary American art. These creative expressions, which take form in as many media as traditional American folk art, spring from

artists living outside the mainstream experiences of most Western cultures. What does this mean? In Europe this type of art is often called Art Brut. Whether Art Brut or Outsider Art, it is art made by individuals who are either mentally or emotionally challenged and therefore living in an institutional setting, like Adolf Wolfli and Martin Ramirez. It is artists whose physical abilities cause them to process and understand information differently from a fully-abled person. For example, Down Syndrome has precluded fiber artist Judith Scott from hearing or speaking. The absence of these senses alters her reception and communication of information. Though her creative need is no different from anyone else's, her concept of sculpture is not based on the same information as artists who can hear and speak. In America, life "outside" the mainstream can be as simple and complex a matter as race and economics. Bill Traylor, an African-American artist working in the South in the 1930s and 1940s who is now

Carved Spread Wing Eagle c. 1890, Carlisle, Pennsylvania, by Wilhelm Schimmel. Hand-carved pine in red paint with cream and black dotted body and yellow beak, crown and feet on rock on a carved base. 13" wingspan. 7 1/4" H × 8" D Photo courtesy David Wheatcroft Antiques

considered a giant of the Outsider aesthetic, was born into slavery and worked in a low-income factory job. By the time he began producing art as an older man, he slept on a wooden pallet bed in a Montgomery, Alabama, funeral home, sitting outside every day to draw his kinetic, abstract images of life, people, and animals on cardboard. More so than traditional American folk art, the Outsider tradition is especially fueled by religious conviction. The works of Edgar Tolson, James Hampton, Elijah Pierce, Sister Gertrude Morgan, Clementine Hunter, Howard Finster, and William Edmondson, to name only a few, are charged with an evangelical passion that brings a missionary element to their work.

History of the American Folk Art Market

Interest in the material of America's past existed in the United States before those goods had even faded from cultural memory. By the centennial celebration of 1876, romantic notions of Betsy Ross, spinning wheels, and the Sons of Liberty, fueled by such salesmen of the Colonial Revival as Wallace Nutting, were well established in American popular culture. While a market for reproductions soon existed, some areas of the country had never stopped producing certain wares for them to be reproduced. The Medingers of Bucks County still made redware pottery just as they had for the previous century; elsewhere in Pennsylvania, Wilhelm Schimmel bartered his

One-Drawer Blanket Chest Early nineteenth century, New England. paint-decorated pine lift-top chest with scalloped front and raised feet. 33" H × 45" W × 18" D Photo courtesy Ballyhack Antiques

carved and painted animal figures for sustenance as others had before him. He then taught the craft to Aaron Mountz. To the north in Maine, John Haley Bellamy carved dramatic, patriotic figures of eagles and banners for the ship building industry, an established area tradition.

More scholarly focus on the art of America's folk began shortly after America's centennial celebration sparked our national imagination. Individuals such as Henry Chapman Mercer, Edwin Atlee Barber, Henry Davis Sleeper, and Edna Greenwood were among the first champions of America's past, guiding an early market through the precedent of their own collections and publications. While a few antiques dealers specialized in Americana at this time, the number of retailers at the turn of the nineteenth and twentieth centuries was nowhere near the quantity that exists today. Interested nascent collectors picked up objects from individuals selling from their farms or small country auctions as much as from any other source. The economic and life cycles of people willing to part with family heirlooms at a time when those goods were still considered old-fashioned, out of date, or valueless vestiges of another generation were early collecting opportunities. While the efforts of advocates like Mercer, Barber, Sleeper, and Greenwood remain today at the Mercer Museum/Bucks County Historical Society in Doylestown, Pennsylvania, the Philadelphia Museum of Art's Pennsylvania German Collection, the Society for the Preservation of New En-

Two-Drawer Dower Chest
c. 1830, Pennsylvania. Lift-top blanket chest on circular turned tapering legs with all-over grain painted decoration in the form of owl's eyes on the front and stylized tulips on the sides. 29" H × 46" W × 23" D. Private collection

gland Antiquities, and the Smithsonian Institution's American History collections, the impact of these individuals was nonetheless local rather than national.

As a field of interest and study, and as a discernible force in the marketplace, American folk art came into its own on a national level during the early twentieth century. Its arrival on the scene is inextricably linked with America's rise internationally as a major influence in the direction of contemporary art. What piqued the interest of collectors, dealers, and artists was the 1913 Armory Show in New York City, an exhibition that presented contemporary American and European art in the same venue and, in so doing, challenged many viewers and participants to find the source of America's artistic heritage. Probably the most important figures in establishing public interest and a national market for American folk art, as well as identifying it as the root of modern American art, were Gertrude Vanderbilt Whitney, Juliana Force, Edith Gregor Halpert, Holger Cahill, Abby Aldrich Rockefeller, and Electra Havemeyer Webb. The impact of these individuals resonates today.

The Whitney Studio Club

In 1914, Gertrude Vanderbilt Whitney (1875–1942) formed a group called Friends of the Young Artists, an organization dedicated to promoting the work of living American artists. In 1918 this group evolved into the

Whitney Studio Club, a similar organization with the added bonus of exhibiting Mrs. Whitney's personal art collection. Developed, guided, and managed by Juliana Force (1876–1948), Mrs. Whitney's assistant, the Whitney Studio Club not only sponsored up-and-coming artists, but refreshed interest in past American artists, such as Winslow Homer and Robert Feke, while being one of the first institutions to endorse American abstract art. In 1924, the Whitney Studio Club was also the first entity to dedicate an exhibition to American folk art and in 1930 became the museum we know today, the Whitney Museum of American Art. Ultimately, the museum chose to focus on its founding mission, promoting contemporary, rather than historical, American art. Fifty years after that first exhibition of American folk art, and in anticipation of the nation's bicentennial celebration, the Whitney Museum launched one of the most important exhibitions on the subject. In 1974, the museum once again brought academia and America up to speed with each other with the opening of the nationwide traveling exhibition, *The Flowering of American Folk Art, 1776–1876*. While the goal of the exhibition and catalog was a re-analysis of the material in light of new scholarship, the effect was a wake-up call to the marketplace.

Abby Aldrich Rockefeller, Holger Cahill, and Edith Gregor Halpert

Like her contemporary, Gertrude Vanderbilt Whitney, Abby Aldrich Rockefeller (1874–1948) was also interested in progressive American art. New York City's arts community at this time was a small and interconnected group of curators, dealers, and buyers who fed and encouraged each other's interests. Through Mrs. Rockefeller's efforts, New York City's Museum of Modern Art was founded in 1929, with Alfred H. Barr Jr., as its first director. Barr soon imported Holger Cahill (1887–1960), whom he knew from the Newark Museum, another institution popularizing modern art. Cahill's landmark 1930 exhibition *American Primitives: An Exhibit of the Paintings of American Folk Artists*, followed in 1931 by *American Folk Sculpture: The Art of Eighteenth and Nineteenth Century Craftsmen,* were nationally traveling shows that placed American folk art at the forefront of American art conversation. At the Museum of Modern

Art, where Cahill was soon acting director, he quickly mounted two more groundbreaking exhibitions: *American Folk Art: Art of the Common Man, 1750–1900*, in 1932, and *American Sources of Modernism* in 1933. These exhibitions squarely placed American folk art, along with recent European academic work, at the root of modern art. Following his work at the Museum of Modern Art, Cahill went on to lead the Works Progress Administration's Federal Art Project, a government subsidized program to support American artists struggling during the Depression. This was also an initiative to codify American art. Among the results of this support and codification was *The Index of American Design*. (See Appendix, Books & Magazines, General, Clarence P. Hornung.)

Cahill directly experienced the connection between American contemporary artists and folk art. Visiting Hamilton Easter Field's artists' colony in Ogunquit, Maine, in 1926, Cahill saw how American folk art inspired visiting artists. Field had decorated the shacks and cottages in which artists and guests resided with hooked rugs, primitive portraits, wind toys, eighteenth and nineteenth century country furniture, and other examples of American folk art, which exemplified the kind of graphic minimalism to which post–World War I artists aspired. Among the contemporary artists whose work was imbued with an American folk sensibility were sculptor Elie Nadelman and painters Charles Sheeler, Marsden Hartley, Stuart Davis, and Yasuo Kuniyoshi, among others. Artists working in Field's colony observed how the various handling of perspective, proportion, figural detail, light, and traditional spatial relationships in American folk art informed their own output. Cahill's passion for modern American art and American folk art and his role at the Museum of Modern Art placed him in a unique position to advise Mrs. Rockefeller. Calling on the talents of contemporary American art dealer Edith Gregor Halpert (1900–1970), who also visited the artists' colony in Ogunquit, Cahill had an immediate source of fresh, new American art, as well as the benefit of Halpert's exceptional eye and efficiency for Mrs. Rockefeller.

Edith Gregor Halpert, a businesswoman by training, started dealing art by opening The Downtown Gallery in 1926. Like the nearby Whitney Studio Club, The Downtown Gallery dedicated itself to showing current art by living American artists without reference to style or school. Halpert's business functioned as much as a cultural center as an art gallery, including discussions with artists and educational programs, some of which were led by Cahill. As Halpert's description of the works in her gallery stated, "Its selection is driven by quality—by what is enduring—not by what is in vogue." Abby Aldrich Rockefeller first visited the Downtown Gallery in 1928, and with Mrs. Rockefeller as her primary patron, sales of American folk art largely supported exhibitions of contemporary American artists and saw The Downtown Gallery through the Depression. In 1929, Holger Cahill encouraged Halpert to open The American Folk Art Gallery, which eventually found permanent residence on the second floor of The Downtown Gallery's Greenwich Village location. The American Folk Art Gallery was the first major gallery dedicated entirely to the subject. In addition to Abby Aldrich Rockefeller, other folk art collectors who sought the advice and treasures of Halpert's Downtown Gallery were Electra Havemeyer Webb, Max and Martha Codman Karolik, and Edgar and Bernice Chrysler Garbisch. Halpert's personal collection of American folk art was, at one time, an intended gift to the Smithsonian Institution. Instead, it was sold at auction by Sotheby's New York in 1973.

The partnership of Edith Gregor Halpert and Holger Cahill had lasting impact on the American art scene of the early and mid-twentieth century. At the same time Cahill was launching exhibitions of American folk art at the Newark Museum, Halpert was doing the same at The Downtown Gallery. While Cahill promoted the scholarly connection between American folk art and modern art, Halpert's 1931 exhibition, *American Ancestors*, linked the emerging markets and collectors of the two. Between Cahill and Halpert, Mrs. Rockefeller had the two best advisers at the forefront of American art. Beyond major additions of American modernism to Mrs. Rockefeller's personal collection, many of which went to the Museum of Modern Art, the American public was also the beneficiary of Mrs. Rockefeller's American folk art collection. The Abby Aldrich Rockefeller Folk Art Center at Colonial Williamsburg, America's most popular living history museum created through the vision and altruism of Abby and her husband John D. Rockefeller Jr., remains one of the foremost institutions and collections of American folk art today.

The Shelburne Museum

Electra Havemeyer Webb (1888–1960) was also born into a wealthy New York City family which, like the Vanderbilts, was an established patron of the arts. Webb's parents, Louisine and Henry O. Havemeyer, were among the first Americans to collect Impressionist paintings, a daring and avant-garde style of work in its time; and the family's relationship with American expatriate Impressionist painter, Mary Cassat, is well documented. Electra Havemeyer Webb was no less a maverick in her own collecting tastes than her parents were. Shortly after her father's death in 1907 had left her a sizable inheritance, and several years before the Armory Show riveted attention on American art and heritage, Webb collected her first example of American folk art, a cigar store figure bought in Stamford, Connecticut. Over the next forty years, she filled her country home in Shelburne, Vermont, with other examples of America's rural past. Objects that belonged inside a home were not enough for Webb, who collected entire buildings as well. Webb established her collection as a museum in 1947; by the time it was opened to the public in 1952 as the Shelburne Museum, Webb had amassed 39 buildings on 45 acres of property. On Webb's death in 1960, the museum had more than 80,000 objects in its collection; the number of objects has since almost doubled.

Like Gertrude Vanderbilt Whitney and Abby Aldrich Rockefeller, Electra Havemeyer Webb saw American folk art in the context of all American art. Folk art was not relegated to a subcategory of American art the way it frequently is today; rather, American folk art stood its ground equally with all the artistic achievements of its native country. In keeping with this vision, the Webb Gallery of American Painting at Shelburne shows anonymous American folk paintings alongside such known artists as Andrew Wyeth, Grandma Moses, Albert Bierstadt, and Winslow Homer. Webb took this vision of American art further than any other collector of her day and was one of the first to display American quilts on a wall as art rather than on a bed as furnishings.

Webb's purchases shared other commonalities with the collectors of her day. Holger Cahill was well known to Mrs. Webb; "Nine Pins," a set of figural carved bowling pins that was one of the stars of Cahill's 1931 Newark Museum traveling exhibition, *American Folk Sculpture*, was in Webb's collection. Webb's art advisers included Edith Gregor Halpert, who provided Webb with as many superlative examples of American contemporary and folk art as she did Mrs. Rockefeller; Halpert eventually served on the board of the Shelburne Museum. As with many collectors, Webb was also concerned with price and value. A painting by Edward Hicks depicting *Penn's Treaty with the Indians, 1681*, done circa 1840 and one of about fifteen known versions by the artist, became available to Webb via Halpert in the 1950s. "I hate to pay that much for a Pennsylvania painting," Webb wrote to Halpert of the $5,000 asking price.[6] Edward Hicks is better known to many today as the artist of *The Peaceable Kingdom*, an allegorical scene of which Hicks painted approximately sixty; a record price at auction for that work was set in 1999 at $4.7 million. More recently in 2000, the highest price paid at auction for a *Penn's Treaty* was $635,000. While Webb's concern seems absurd in today's marketplace, her observation shows how far the market has come from the time she began collecting and in the half century since.

The experiences of these three pioneering collectors reveal several insights into the history of the American folk art market. First, its beginnings lay in the emerging modern American art market. In addition to professionals like Cahill and Halpert forging this connection, others did as well, such as legendary art dealer Sidney Janus and collector Albert Barnes. Second, implicit in its connection to contemporary American art is that American folk art had an aspect of modernity to it well beyond its aesthetic. Just as historical folk art informed some American artists' contemporary style, the art of the common man was not necessarily all historical. Grandma Moses, Ho-

[6] Grace Glueck, Sept 6 2003, http://www.azcentral.com/ent/arts/articles/0906folkart06.html

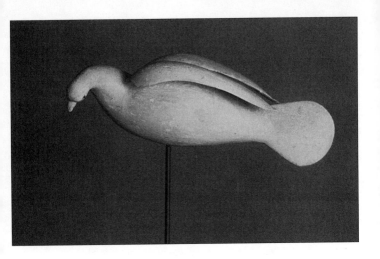

Carved Wooden Dove
Early twentieth century, found in Michigan. With old painted finish. 13" L
Photo courtesy American Primitive Galley

race Pippin, Patsy Santo, Morris Hirschfield, Ralph Fasanella, William Edmondson, and Bill Traylor were all artists working in the twentieth century in a folk tradition. As a result of the awareness that folk art continues, these artists all saw their work appreciated within their lifetimes. With the exception of Grandma Moses, however, all of these artists subsequently faded from discussion, only to be rediscovered recently.[7]

The third and most enduring effect of these early collectors was the setting of a standard for future American folk art buyers. In the quality, quantity, and relative expense of the objects they acquired, early collectors created a canon of American folk art: some objects or artists were more rare; certain regions of the country were more collectible than others; some time periods were more desirable than others. During the early part of the twentieth century, the essential guiding principle of major folk art collections was generally that objects from the nineteenth century were better than those from the twentieth century; that New England was the treasure chest of the nation; and that American folk art was primarily a rural rather than an urban expression. While gaps in logic can be easily pointed out in these conclusions, disciples of that first generation of American folk art collectors

[7] Richard Guy Wilson, "Contemporary American Folk Art: Charming Junk or Art with a Capital A?" http://www.virginia.edu/artmuseum/ VirtualExhibitions/folk/essay.html

nonetheless went forth buying with a nineteenth-century, rural New England directive in mind. As a second generation Americana collector, Nina Fletcher Little wrote in her introduction to the first published catalog of Mrs. Rockefeller's folk art collection, "New England was the richest center of folk art because it was richest in craftsmen . . . in the South there is less evidence of folk art."[8] Today, although we know all three assumptions of time, outlook, and place to be products of that era of collecting, these distinctions have had an enduring effect on our appreciation of the aesthetics of American folk art.

Time and geography are the two assumptions that remain most prevalent in our current differentiation between traditional and nontraditional American folk art. While New England has been replaced by the East Coast, the nineteenth century remains a chronological barrier after which many more traditional collectors do not collect. Late nineteenth-century urban weathervanes, shop figures, carousel art, and trade signs have removed the stigma of the city from American folk art's previously rural implication. Western American folk art influenced by North America's Spanish settlers, such as Santos figures, are relatively recent arrivals to the discussion of the subject. Likewise, Outsider Art, which has an inherently contemporary, urban, sometimes unreal, or even dreamlike feel to it, is predicated on ideals inherently antithetical to what the marketplace came to define as classic folk art.

Where this book focuses on marketplace definitions because they tend to be more practical for the beginning collector, it would be an oversight not to survey the academic evolution of the American folk art field. With the advent of such important institutions as the Whitney Museum, the Abby Aldrich Rockefeller Folk Art Center, the Shelburne Museum, the American Folk Art Museum, and additions of American folk art to collections not solely focused on folk art, such as the Winterthur, the Metropolitan Museum of Art, and the Museum of Fine Arts, Boston, academia has had to come to terms with this often difficult and definition-defying material as well. While academicians have led the charge to understand

[8] Nina Fletcher Little, *The Abby Rockefeller Folk Art Collection* (Boston: Little, Brown & Company, 1957), xiv.

American folk art from an art historical, social historical, or anthropological framework, collectors and dealers have championed a more qualitative, connoisseurship-driven means of assessing the material, leading to the conclusion that academia and the marketplace have parted company. The difference between the two approaches to appreciating American folk art can be summed up as simply as the difference between the two questions: What makes American folk art? And, what makes good American folk art? While many institutions offer courses on American folk art or have hosted symposia on the subject, the divergence of these two schools of thought came to a head in November 1977 at a conference held by the Winterthur Museum. The four-part event, a conference, exhibition, catalog, and published report surrounded "Beyond Necessity: Art in the Folk Tradition," an exhibition put together by the Winterthur and held at the Brandywine River Museum in Chadds Ford, Pennsylvania. Attendance grew to a capacity of 390 people, and at a fee of $25 per person, the symposium was quickly filled. According to subsequent reports of the conference, many attendees, mostly dealers and collectors, felt that the conference didn't address the material as much as its social context, and even that was done in overwrought terms.[9] The conference begged the question, which has yet to be answered academically: Can American folk art be appreciated and valued on its own terms and for what it is, or is its value purely in its social history?

In addition to Gertrude Vanderbilt Whitney, Juliana Force, Edith Gregor Halpert, Holger Cahill, Abby Aldrich Rockefeller, and Electra Havemeyer Webb, many others shaped our present knowledge and understanding of American folk art. Some of these were great collectors who taught through their museum bequests or through the auction catalogs that documented and dispersed their collection to a new generation of buyers. Others were dealers, editors, authors, and curators. Our understanding of American folk art is as much molded by its earlier and more recent custodians as it is by the people

[9] *The Gray Letter*, Vol. II, No. 48 (Boone, Inc., Tuscaloosa, Alabama), December 12, 1977.

who created the objects originally. Since provenance can be so important to understanding an object, the following account lists a few of the major twentieth-century collectors, auctions, and educators in the field of American folk art whose names you need to know. In the interest of privacy, current collectors—today's living legends of the American folk art market—have been excluded, unless their collection was auctioned and constituted a landmark sale.

Legendary Collectors

George Horace Lorimer (1867–1937) was best known for his stewardship of *The Saturday Evening Post*. He was as enthusiastic about American folk art as he was accurate in measuring the tastes of his American readership. His collection of European and American art was sold at auction at Parke-Bernet Galleries in New York City in two parts in 1944.

Elie Nadelman (1882–1946) was a Polish sculptor who immigrated to the United States. He collected American folk art and exhibited the collection at his home, Alderbrook, in Riverdale, New York. Due to financial reversals, the Nadelman folk art collection was sold at auction at Anderson Galleries in New York City in 1935–37.

Henry Francis du Pont (1880–1969) was the Wilmington, Delaware, collector who remodeled and expanded his family home north of Wilmington into what is now the Winterthur Museum and Gardens, a 175-room period museum that opened in 1951. Displaying more than 85,000 objects made between 1640 and 1860, the Winterthur has among the foremost museum collections of American decorative arts in the country.

Francis (1875–1937) and **Mabel Brady Garvan** were avid collectors of formal high-end American furniture, and collected some folk and vernacular forms as well. A graduate of the Yale College class of 1897, Garvan left his collection to Yale University in honor of his wife.

Titus C. Geesey (d. 1969) was a Wilmington, Delaware, collector influential in establishing the holdings of American art at the Delaware Art Museum and, most notably, the Philadelphia Museum of Art. In 1969, Geesey gave

Wooden Figure of Man, Early twentieth century, New England. Constructed of a carved wooden tree trunk with articulated arms and legs, retaining original polychrome finish. Approximately 6' 6" H Provenance: Formerly Dorothea & Leo Rabkin Collection; now in the collection of the American Folk Art Museum, New York

his collection of Pennsylvania German arts to the Philadelphia Museum of Art. These went on display starting in 1958, his art formed the core of the museum's Pennsylvania German holdings.

Stewart E. Gregory (1914–1976) was one in the waves of secondary American folk art collectors who was guided by dealer Mary Allis. When Sotheby's sold the well-recognized Gregory collection in 1979, many of the individual items set a number of auction records, including those for paintings, sculpture, and weathervanes.

Eleanor (dates unknown) and **Mabel Van Alstyne** (c. 1882–1965) amassed a collection of American folk art in the early and mid-twentieth century including carousel figures, Southern pottery, weathervanes, and scrimshaw. In 1964, Mabel Van Alstyne donated the collection to the Smithsonian Institution's National Museum of American History.

Dr. Albert C. Barnes (1872–1951) collected what he considered masterpieces, whether seventeenth-century Old Masters, Impressionist paintings, American folk art, or more contemporary works of art, freely mixing European masters, such as Rubens, Renoir, and Modigliani, with modern American artists, like Horace Pippin.

Ima Hogg (1882–1975) began collecting American art and antiques in the 1920s. Her collection focused on American decorative arts and some classic folk art, such as needlework. In 1966, she gave her collection and the house in which it was displayed, Bayou Bend, to the Museum of Fine Arts, Houston.

Martha Codman (1858–1948) and **Maxim Karolik** (1893–1963) collected in three categories of American art: furniture and decorative arts, paintings, and watercolors. In 1939, the Karoliks gave their collection to the Museum of Fine Arts, Boston. Among the important folk art treasures in the gift are Erastus Salisbury Field's large portrait of Joseph Moore and his family.

Edgar William (1899–1980) and **Bernice Chrysler Garbisch** (1907–1980) collected classic American folk art, which is now dispersed among the National Gallery of Art, the Metropolitan Museum of Art, and the Whitney Museum of American Art (many of the Whitney donations were later sold at Sotheby's in the 1990s). The remainder of the Garbisch's collection was sold in four parts in January, May, and November 1974 by Sotheby Parke-Bernet (now Sotheby's) on site at the Garbisch's home, Pokety, on Maryland's Eastern Shore.

Bertram K. (1899–1993) and **Nina Fletcher Little** (1903–1993) were the nephew and niece-in-law of Edna Greenwood. The Littles collected New England decorative arts and folk art. Bertram Little was director of the Society for the Preservation of New England Antiquities, to which much of their estate was left. Nina Fletcher Little's publications, including the first catalog of the Abby Aldrich Rockefeller Folk Art Center's collection, placed her among the foremost scholars of her generation. The remainder of their collection was sold over two sales at Sotheby's New York in January and October 1994.

Howard (1905–1993) and **Jean Lipman** (1912–1990) collected diverse works of art from contemporary sculpture to classic American folk art. Mrs. Lipman was editor of *Art in America* for 30 years, and the Lipmans' generosity in dispersing their collection included the Whitney Museum and the American Folk Art Museum. The latter gift was intended for sale to benefit the museum, after it had chosen what it wanted of the Lipmans' property. This sale took place at Sotheby's New York in 1981.

Bert Hemphill (1929–1998) focused on contemporary American folk art. A founding member in 1961 of what is now the American Folk Art Museum, Hemphill was its first curator. In 1986, the National Museum of American Art acquired Hemphill's collection, and auctioned its remainder at Sotheby's New York and Slotin Folk Art in Georgia during the 1990s.

Paint-Decorated Shaker Sewing Desk
c. 1820–30, from Enfield, New Hampshire.
35 1/2" H × 38 3/4" W × 26 3/4" D
Provenance: The collection of Edward Deming
and Faith Andrews
Illustrated: *Shaker Furniture, The
Craftsmanship of an American Communal Sect*,
Edward Deming and Faith Andrews, Plate #32,
page 88. *The Complete Book of Shaker Furniture*,
Timothy Reiman & Jean Burks, Plate #207,
page 252. *The Shaker Legacy, Perspectives on
an Enduring Furniture Style*, Christian
Becksvoort, Page 187.
Photo courtesy John Keith Russell Antiques

Great Advocates

The following individuals are collectors, editors, curators, dealers, or other professionals in the field of American folk art. While their achievements were many, their greatest accomplishments were promoting and disseminating information about American folk art, whether through scholarship or the marketplace.

James Abbe Jr. (1912–1999) was an accomplished fashion photographer whose artistic aesthetic was influenced by his well-known photographer father and by his own skills. In 1961 he left photography and became a dealer in American folk art and paintings. He had stores in Oyster Bay and Easthampton, New York. He was a founding member of the American Folk Art Museum.

Mary Allis (1899–1987), active from the 1950s through the 1980s and considered the matriarch of the folk art painting field, was located in Southport, Connecticut. Never one to be intimidated, Mary Allis was legendary in helping form major collections of American folk art and in influencing many prominent dealers who then went on to form other collections.

Faith (1887–1990) and **Edward Deming Andrews** (1894–1964) were dealers, collectors, and authors who popularized Shaker design in the 1920s. In *Religion in Wood*, one of their many publications, they promoted the notion that the religious ideals of the Shakers were directly expressed in their furniture design. Although recent studies have largely debunked many of the Andrews' theories about Shaker aesthetic motivation and Shaker retention of agrarian materials, the Andrewses nonetheless were the first and most successful champions of these nineteenth-century forms that appealed to twentieth-century eyes.

Ruth (dates unknown) and **Roger Bacon** (dates unknown) were legendary New Hampshire dealers active in the middle part of the twentieth century who focused on decorative arts from the seventeenth and eighteenth centuries. This dynamic duo brought drama to the field of early furniture.

Edith (dates unknown) and **Bernard Barenholtz** (1914–1989), active in the 1960s and 1970s, were St. Louis natives who moved to Princeton, New Jersey. Bernard was the genius behind Creative Playthings, one of the first educational toy companies in the 1960s. He and Edith shared a passion for collecting tin toys and mechanical banks. This led them to American decorative arts, and they formed one of the mid-twentieth century's most important collections of American folk art.

Preston Bassett (c. 1902–1984), from Ridgefield, Connecticut, collected outstanding examples of American folk art, especially in the area of stoneware pottery. His collection now resides in the New York State Museum in Albany.

Robert Bishop (1938–1991) was an author and museum director whose personal magnetism and enthusiasm for American folk art are still felt at the American Folk Art Museum, where Bishop was director for many years.

John Bivins Jr. (1940–2001) was a wood carver, long rifle maker, author, curator, and independent scholar. Bivins' love for North Carolina decorative arts ignored distinctions like 'high end' or 'vernacular.' His groundbreaking work, with Brad Rauschenberg, on Moravian pottery, his work on North Carolina long rifles, and coastal furniture of North Carolina remain the definitive texts on the subject. Bivins's posthumous publication, again with Rauschenberg, on Charleston furniture raised the level of decorative arts scholarship.

Mary Black (1922–1991) was a curator, author, and expert on American folk art whose career and publications included some of the most important mid-twentieth century scholarship on the subject.

Mrs. J. Insley Blair (c. 1940s) was one of the major benefactors of the American Wing at the Metropolitan Museum of Art. A quick look at almost all other important New York City museums shows that her gifts of American furniture and folk and decorative arts to these institutions were also incredibly generous.

Ron Bourgeault, creator of Northeast Auctions in Portsmouth, New Hampshire, is the first regional auctioneer to give the major international auction houses significant competition in several collecting areas including Americana.

Hattie Brunner (1889–1982) was a southeastern Pennsylvania antiques dealer who formed some of the best local collections of Pennsylvania German folk art.

Robert Carlen (1916–1984) was a well-known Philadelphia art dealer who influenced other art dealers by helping to train their eyes. In 1939 Carlen became Horace Pippin's art dealer.

Russell Carrell (1917–1998) was a Salisbury, Connecticut, antiques dealer who started the "Antiques in a Cow Pasture" series of outdoor antiques shows. These purported to be the first antiques shows exhibiting quality antiques outdoors and were patterned after Paris's famous Marché au Puce.

Ed Clerk (d. 1995) was a Shaker dealer who helped build a number of collections. He participated for many years in the prestigious East Side Settlement House Antiques Show in New York City.

Lillian Blankely Cogan (1898–1991) was a Farmington, Connecticut, antiques dealer whose shop, Hearts and Crowns, specialized in seventeenth- and early eighteenth-century American decorative arts and folk art. Following Cogan's death, Christie's New York sold the inventory of her shop in an on-site auction in September 1992.

Henry Coger (1925–2001) was a Massachusetts antiques dealer who, along with **John Bihler** (d.1992), subsequently moved to Dallas, Texas. Coger and Bihler later ran William Griffith Antiques in Dallas, and Coger was one of the founders in 1975 of Dallas's Tri Delta Antiques Show.

Barry Cohen (1935–1990) was a New York City artist and antiques collector who constantly traded with dealers to upgrade his choice collection of American folk art.

Gary C. Cole (dates unknown) began his career as an interior decorator and evolved to become a folk art dealer who was active on the scene in the 1960s and 1970s.

Eric De Jong (d. 1995) was the chief curator of The William Penn Memorial Museum in Harrisburg, Pennsylvania. He wrote and lectured extensively on American folk art, with an emphasis on Pennsylvania German.

William Doyle (1940–1993) was a native Bostonian who became a New York City antiques dealer. A friend of Bob Skinner's, with his tutelage, Doyle successfully founded Doyle Galleries, an auction house in New York City.

Nancy Druckman has a name that is almost as much of a household word as the "stuff" itself. From her post as head of American folk art at Sotheby's New York, she has, for the past 30 years, presided over and directed most of the important auction sales in the field.

Adele Earnest (1901–1993) was a collector and dealer and the author of *Folk Art in America* and several books on American decoys. She also operated the Stony Point Folk Art Gallery in Stony Point, New York, with Cordelia Hamilton (dates unknown). She and Cordy were involved with the Museum of Early American Folk Art, the precursor to today's American Folk Art Museum.

Betty Forbes (b. 1918) and **Frances Phipps** (1924–1986) were the co-managers of The Hartford Antiques Show. During the middle part of the twentieth century, this show was a major source for collectors. Phipps was also involved in many Connecticut historical restoration projects and was author of *Colonial Kitchens: Their Furnishing and Their Gardens.*

Alice Ford (1906–1997) was an editor and a John James Audubon scholar. She was the author of *Edward Hicks: His Life and Art* with Eleanor Price Mather.

Ed Fuller (1941–1985) was a folk art dealer from Woodstock, New York, who was the primary promoter of William Edmondson's stone sculptures.

Rocky (1911–1986) and **Avis Gardiner** (1908–1998) were legendary antiques dealers from Stamford, Connecticut, whose "finds" are now in such museum collections as the Winterthur.

John Gordon (1921–2003) was a folk art dealer in New York City in the middle part of the twentieth century.

Hazel Hayes (active c. 1960s–1980s) was an antiques dealer from Somers, Connecticut, who specialized in Shaker furniture and decorative arts.

Wally and **Margo Jester** (dates unknown), active in the 1940s to the 1960s, were St. Louis dealers who helped form many midwestern collections.

Lou Jones (1908–1990) Director of the Cooperstown graduate program in American folk art who, with his wife, **Agnes,** was one of the most influential people in building scholarship in the field.

Ted Kapnek (d. 1980) began collecting miniatures, discovered American needlework, and became one of the preeminent collectors in that field. His collection was exhibited in 1979 at the American Folk Art Museum in New York City and dispersed at Sotheby's in 1981 following his death. The Theodore H. Kapnek Collection of American Samplers, sold 21 January 1981, brought new focus to needlework and set new highs at auction.

Joe Kindig Jr. (active c. 1940s–1960s), in the early part of the twentieth century, was a legendary Pennsylvania dealer who sold some of the most important examples

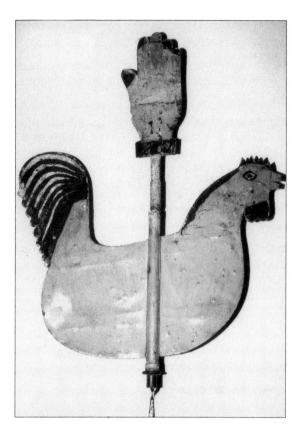

Rooster Weathervane
Early twentieth century, found in Maine. Polychrome sheet iron and wood. Approximately 3' H
Private collection

of Pennsylvania German and Shenandoah Valley furniture and decorative arts to several major collectors including Henry Francis du Pont. The business continues today, run by his son, Joe Kindig III, and granddaughter, Jenifer Kindig.

Eugene King (active c. 1980s) was an antiques dealer from Moline, Illinois, who was almost larger than life. He participated in some of the most significant antiques shows in the country and vied with the best of the dealers even though he was in the Midwest, far from the sales venues of many of the folk art objects he sold.

Gerald Kornblau (active c. 1960s–1980s) was a photographer who began with a small shop on the Upper East Side of New York City. He graduated to be an exhibitor at the prestigious East Side Settlement House Antiques Show, where he was one of the first to spotlight pieces of

American folk art by putting them on pedestals and isolating them as art objects.

Jim Kronen (active c. 1970s) was an extraordinarily active New York City antiques dealer. In the 1980s he was one of the first dealers to display American folk art as art.

Judy Lenett (active c. 1970s–1980s) was a Connecticut folk art dealer whose tactile sensitivity and sensibility were revealed in the objects she chose to sell.

Frances M. Lichten (active c. 1950s): Philadelphia Supervisor of the Index of Design and author whose scholarly publications on Pennsylvania German folk art in the 1940s–1970s brought the material to a wider audience.

Zeke Liverant (1917–2001) was a legendary and beloved Colchester, Connecticut, antiques dealer whose father, Nathan, started the business in 1920. His son Arthur continues the business today.

Florene Maine (1900–1980) was a Ridgefield, Connecticut, antiques dealer specializing in New England country furniture and folk art. Her estate was sold by Sotheby's New York in January 1981.

Alistair Bradley Martin (active c. 1940s–1980s) is the guiding force behind the Guennol Collection, most of which forms the nucleus of the American folk art collection at the Brooklyn Museum in New York City.

Burt Martinson (1911–1970) was a New York City collector who was instrumental in founding the Museum of Early American Folk Art.

Eleanor Price Mather (b. 1910) was an author who, with Alice Ford, wrote one of the first appreciations of nineteenth-century Quaker artist Edward Hicks.

Dorothy Canning Miller (1900–2003) was a curator and author. She was among the early curators at the Museum of Modern Art who included American folk art in exhibitions of American art. The wife of Holger Cahill, Miller was also instrumental in identifying works of American folk art for her husband.

Cyril I. Nelson (active c. 1970s–1980s) is a former editor at E. P. Dutton, New York City. He was instrumental in bringing a great number of the definitive books on collecting and identifying American folk art to fruition during the middle part of the twentieth century. He was the editor for the Quilt Calendars. Nelson hails from a collecting family and is a well-known collector himself.

Harry Shaw Newman (1896–1966) was the second owner of The Old Print Shop in New York City, taking over the business from the widow of founder Edward Gottschalk in 1928. During the 1940s and 1950s, the shop promoted American folk art, though more recently it has redefined its focus on prints and out-of-print art books.

Helena Penrose (active c. 1940s–1950s), based in New York City, was a well known pioneer dealer in American folk art.

Priscilla (1905–1996) and **Howard** (1899–1985) **Richmond** were transplanted New Yorkers working as antiques dealers in Woodbury, Connecticut. They purchased the former home and shop of Helena Penrose. The Richmonds were influential in promoting American country decorative arts.

Howard Rose (1922–1987) was an art collector and dealer who worked at the Downtown and Kennedy galleries in New York City. With Raymond Saroff, he formed a collection discussed in Rose's book, *Unexpected Eloquence: The Art in American Art*, written in the 1970s and published in the 1990s.

Israel Sack (1883–1959) was a cabinetmaker from Lithuania who became a renowned Boston and New York City antiques dealer. His three sons, Harold, Albert, and Robert, continued the business. Over the years, both generations of the Sack family sold some of the most important examples of American furniture and decorative arts. Albert's 1950 book, *Fine Points of Furniture: Early American*, established the "Good, Better, Best" criteria by which many collectors subsequently assessed American furniture. The Sack firm was started in 1903 in Boston, Massachusetts, subsequently moved to New York City, and was then closed when the company inventory was sold at Sotheby's New York in January 2002.

George (c. 1889–1970) and **Mildred Samaha** (1910–1966) were general antiques dealers in Milan, Ohio, who specialized in Midwestern glass. Mildred was influenced to notice American furniture and folk art by Rhea Mansfield Nittle, who was an early adviser to the Garvans and whose husband was a well-known Midwestern auctioneer. Their son, Bill Samaha, continues as a force in the field today.

Norbert and **Gail Savage** (active c. 1960s–1990s) Bert worked in the antiques department at Marshall Field's in Chicago, Illinois, selling American furniture and folk art. Then he and Gail went into business for themselves and helped form and influence many Midwestern collections. After their divorce and until his death in 2002, Bert sold American Adirondack furniture and decorative arts. He was one of the first to recognize this artistic tradition.

George E. Schoellkopf (b. 1948?) moved to New York City from Dallas, Texas, and became a collector who turned into a New York City folk art dealer. He is now a country gentleman.

Clara Endicott Sears (1863–1960) was an early preservationist, collector, author, and founder of the Fruitlands Museum in Harvard, Massachusetts. The Fruitlands Museum is comprised of several structures on one property, each of which is dedicated to a particular theme in American intellectual history and furnished appropriately. The Museum is also, in part, founded on the same property that was the site of Bronson Alcott's eponymous Transcendental community.

Charlotte (1917–1998) and **Edgar** (1900–1985) **Sittig** were Pennsylvania folk art dealers.

Bob Skinner (1933–1984) was an antiques dealer and founder of Skinner, Inc. auction house in Bolton, Massachusetts. Skinner, Inc. has sold many important examples of American folk art.

Betty Sterling (b. 1919), now retired, owned Brainstorm Farm and specialized in extraordinary examples of American folk art. She exhibited at major antiques shows and helped form a number of collections.

Isabel Carleton Wilde (active c. 1940s–1950s) was a pioneering New York City folk art dealer.

Alice Winchester (1908–1997) was the second of only four editors of *The Magazine Antiques*, who led the publication from the end of the Depression into its most popular era in the 1960s and early 1970s. Winchester was also the co-curator, with Jean Lipman, of *The Flowering of American Folk Art,* the exhibition catalog for the Whitney Museum of Art.

Rudolph Wunderlich (active c. 1960s–1970s) was one of the longest standing American art dealers in the United States. Based in Chicago and New York City, the gallery specialized in works of art from the eighteenth through twentieth centuries.

Landmark Sales

The James M. Shoemaker Collection: Illustrated Catalog of Hooked Rugs. Anderson Galleries, New York, 1923. This sale was among the first to bring strong prices for hooked rugs. The sale of one lot for $2,000 made headlines, and the total rug collection brought $20,500.

The Philip Flayderman Sale of Colonial Furniture, Silver, and Decorations, Anderson Art Association, New York, January 1930. This auction was one of the first groundbreaking sales of American decorative arts and folk art. Not only were record prices achieved during this sale but also several objects important to subsequent furniture scholarship came to light.

Estate of Wallace Nutting, Parke-Bernet Galleries, New York, 1941. Nutting was a New England antiquarian, author, photographer, and entrepeneur who was one of the first to market historical American furniture to the American public through reproductions and quaintly staged photographs recreating Colonial American life.

Walter Himmelreich, Pennypacker Auctions, Reading, Pennsylvania, 1950s–1970s. Himmelreich was a noted collector whose focus was mostly Pennsylvania German folk art. The Himmelreich collection(s) were sold over a period of twenty-five years at Pennypacker Auctions.

Haffenreffer Collection of Cigar Store Indians and Other American Trade Signs, Parke-Bernet Galleries, New York, April and October 1956. These auctions were the first sales focusing on American folk sculpture, in particular late nineteenth century advertising art, such as trade signs and tobacconist figures.

Estate of Arthur J. Sussel, Parke-Bernet Galleries, New York, 1958–1959. This was the first landmark sale to include Pennsylvania German folk art.

Helena Penrose, Parke-Bernet Galleries, New York, February 1960. This was the first major sale of a variety of late nineteenth- and early twentieth-century fairground, maritime, and advertising sculpture including carousel figures, trade signs, and ship figureheads.

John Kenneth Byard, Parke-Bernet Galleries, New York, March 1960. The sale included and set high prices for American drawings, paintings, quilts, and folk art.

William J. Mackey, Jr., Richard A. Bourne Auctions, Belford, New Jersey, July 1973. This sale was one of the first landmark collections of American duck decoys to fetch high prices at auction.

Mr. and Mrs. Christopher Huntington, Morrill's Auctions, Mount Vernon, Maine, June 1974. Chris Huntington was a well-respected antiques dealer. This sale in 1974 was one of the first auctions to realize high prices for paint-decorated furniture.

Mr. and Mrs. Charles B. Hagler Collection of American Stoneware Pottery, Kinzle Auction Center, Duncansville, Pennsylvania, August 1975. This auction was one of the first in which American stoneware brought high prices.

Estate of Henry J. Kauffman, Conestoga Auctions, Manheim, Pennsylvania, May 1977. This sale was among the first of several increasingly important sales of Pennsylvania German folk art and decorative arts starting with the Himmelreich sales.

Stewart E. Gregory Sale, Sotheby Parke Bernet, New York, January 1979. This sale set high prices and some records for exceptional examples of American folk art and paint-decorated furniture.

Helen Janssen Wetzel, Sotheby's, on site in Tulpehocken Farm, Pennsylvania, September 1980. This sale was another auction benchmark for Pennsylvania German folk art.

Collection of Donald and Faye Walters, Sotheby's New York, October 1980. The sale from the personal collection of Don Walters, a former Abby Aldrich Rockefeller folk art curator-turned-dealer, brought strong prices for hard-to-find American folk art.

The Barbara Johnson Collection of Scrimshaw and Related Whaling Material, Sotheby's New York, in three parts, the most significant sale of which was in December 1981. This sale set a number of high prices for American marine and whaling folk art.

Fred Wichmann Sale, Sotheby's New York, June 1983. This was another sale with high prices for Pennsylvania German folk art.

Estate of Hillary Underwood, Sotheby's New York, October 1983. Underwood was a well-respected dealer in Woodstock, Vermont. Her sale brought strong prices for New England folk art.

Collection of Peter Tillou, Sotheby's New York, October 1985. This well-respected dealer's collection brought healthy prices for American folk portraits, paintings, and drawings.

M. Austin and Jill R. Fine, Sotheby's New York, January 1987. In addition to its selection of classic American folk art, the Fine sale was the first auction to sell a Baltimore Album quilt for a record price of $176,000.

Howard and Catherine Feldman, Sotheby's New York, June 1988. The Feldman Collection offered a wide selection of good, classic American folk art to the marketplace. Less remarkable for the objects themselves, the prices were healthy across the board.

Bernard Barenholtz, Sotheby's, New York, January 1989. This sale set the auction record for an American weathervane, a stamped J. Howard and Company horse and rider weathervane that sold for $770,000.

Fish Lamp
Early twentieth century, Michigan. Polychrome carved wooden and tin oil lamp in the form of a fish, converted to a table lamp. Approximately 16" H
Provenance: Robert Bishop; Private collection

Dr. Earl F. Robacker and Ada F. Robacker, Horst Auctions, Ephrata, Pennsylvania, May–August 1989. Collectors and scholars, the Robackers' sales are considered landmarks that set exceptional prices for Pennsylvania German folk art.

Burton and Helaine Fendelman, Sotheby's New York, October 1993. Like the Huntington sale in 1974, the Fendelman sale recalibrated the market for high-quality paint-decorated American furniture.

Pennsylvania German Folk Art from the Collection of Mr. and Mrs. George M. Scott, Christie's, on-site in Lancaster, Pennsylvania, June 1994. In addition to the high prices achieved for Pennsylvania German folk art, this sale brought trade and national media attention to Pennsylvania German makers of folk art and witnessed the arrival of another major and non-local auction house to the competition for sales of these otherwise regional goods.

The Estate of Dr. Henry J. Deyerle, Sotheby's, on-site in Charlottesville, Virginia, May 1995. This auction set the record price for an American paint-decorated blanket chest; a Johannes Spitler chest sold for $343,500 to Colonial Williamsburg. The auction also was one of the first to introduce Southern American folk art to a predominantly Northern collecting community.

Collection of the Late H. William Koch, Pook & Pook, on-site in Turbotville, Pennsylvania, June 1999. This third and final sale of Koch's collection set auction records for several American folk art forms and brought staggering prices for others. Among the auction records set was $687,500 for a Jacob Maentel watercolor family portrait and $181,500 for a single fraktur birth certificate by Daniel Otto. A book containing seven full-page fraktur drawings, two full-page folk art drawings, and fourteen smaller folk art drawings brought $198,000; three Charles Hoffman paintings brought $253,000 (twice) and $209,000.

The Estate of Clark and Mary Garrett, Mike Clum Auctions, Rushville, Ohio, June 2002. Clark Garrett was a well-respected Americana collector/dealer. The June 2002 sale was the last of four sales of the Garretts' property following their deaths in the 1980s. Given how long much of the property had been off the market, and its overall qual-

Crazy Quilt
c. 1890,
Kentucky.
Pieced and
embroidered
quilt in cotton
and silk.
68" × 62".
Photo courtesy
Shelly Zegart
1970s:
$75–$125
1980s:
$5,500–$7,500
Today:
$3,500–$5,500

ity, top prices were reached for superlative works, such as $250,000 for a full-length William Matthew Prior oil on canvas portrait of a boy with a whip and $250,000 for a paint-decorated Pennsylvania schrank.

Current Market Trends

The danger in including a summary of great folk art sales since the 1920s is that for some, it may imply that auctions of American folk art are always successful. Looking at auctions of American folk art generally, this is not the case. Over the last fifteen years in New York City alone, auctions of American folk art have run at a fluctuating success rate. Sometimes as little as 50% of the property offered in an American folk art auction is sold to a new owner and 50% of the property remained unsold and was returned to its consignor. Within the 50% that sold, there are further breakdowns of how well the property sold relative to its estimate—did it sell above, within, or below the anticipated figure when the auction house chose to publish one? Auction results throughout the country have fluctuated over the years. Though in some instances, objects that would not have sold well in New York City have sold for very competitive prices in country auctions close to where they were made.

Taking a few examples—a weathervane, a crazy quilt, and two portraits—and looking at how these objects have fared in value over the last thirty years is literally an object lesson in current market trends and how to con-

"Portrait of Mary Margaret Deuel"
Early nineteenth century, probably New York, by Ammi Phillips (1788–1865). Oil on canvas.
1970s: $3,500
1980s: $90,000
Today: $125,000
Photo courtesy Skinner, Inc.

Cotton H. & Harriet Foss Portraits
Dated March 22, 1836, New England, by Joseph H. Davis (1811–1865). Watercolor on paper. 1970s: $750–$1,000 pr.
1980s: $1,500–$1,800 pr.
Today: $15,000–$20,000 pr.
Photo courtesy Skinner, Inc.

sider the American folk art market going forward. Using auction records of similar material with each object, we have stated approximate appraisal values appropriate for the 1970s, the 1980s, and today.

Generally speaking, American folk art has risen considerably in value; certain sectors of the marketplace, however, have declined. In the 1980s, the quilt market was very hot and exceptional examples of this textile

art were sold for equally exceptional prices. Today, it is very unusual for a quilt to bring big money at auction, though it has happened. Since quilts require specific care, shouldn't be exposed to light, and are difficult to display, readily available inexpensive modern reproductions that are easily cared for have removed an important layer of buyers from the competition for these objects. Likewise, portraits were a hot commodity in the 1980s as well. Today, with the exception of a few works by a few artists, most portraits are not selling for what they did fifteen years ago. In contrast, weathervanes, needlework and Pennsylvania German folk art have all seen tremendous gains in value.

The purpose of these examples is to show that some objects rise in value and some objects decline in value. There is no way to know in which direction any given collecting area will go. As we have stated elsewhere, the best way to buy American folk art is with your heart and your eye, not your investment funds. ◼

Eagle Weathervane
Mid-nineteenth century, New England. Cast iron sheet metal in the form of a winged eagle with shield. Approximately $5^{1}/_{2}$' H × 4' W
1970s: $550
1980s: $7,500
Today: $15,000
Photo courtesy American Folk Art Museum

5

COLLECTING AMERICAN FOLK ART RECORDS AND MORE

To understand the prices fetched for American folk art in the marketplace, it is important to place those prices in context and define the parameters of their sales.

The majority of American folk art is modestly priced, and many dealers are willing to work out extended payment plans for budget-conscious buyers who nonetheless want an original work of art. Some righteous examples of American folk art can be had for as little as a few hundred dollars. Bear in mind, however, that generally speaking, you get what you pay for: A work of art priced at the more modest end of the marketplace is more likely than not to remain there. Although it has happened, comparatively few works of art escalate in value so vastly that one can predict with any accuracy what will or will not rise in value. As we have stated previously, buying with your heart, not with your portfolio, is the only way to approach this market.

While the cap on 90% of the American folk art market is $100,000 and most examples sell well below that, a few exceptional objects have set record prices greatly in excess of that $100,000 mark. In discussing American folk art in terms of good, better, and best, it's important to understand how those qualifications translate to dollars.

American Folk Art Records

The following auction records presently exist for various examples of American folk art. In some instances, we have included second- and third-highest prices paid at auction. We have also included more general values to show the full range of prices possible for a given object. Note that the majority of objects of a specific type generally sell at the more modest end—everyone wants to believe the antique they have found is a hidden treasure. Sadly, this is usually not the case. All auction prices listed include a buyer's premium ranging from 10% to 19.5% on the first $100,000 and 10% thereafter, depending on when and where the object was sold at auction.

Sculpture
Carousel Figures

One of the more popular and recently collected areas of American folk art is carousel figures. These lively and often elaborately decorated, bejeweled creatures are sometimes based on real animals such as horses (most common), goats, cats, dogs, rabbits, pigs, giraffes, and lions, among others, and sometimes based on fantastical beasts like sea serpents. Carousel figures come in an array of positions and with a discernible degree of decoration based on their location on the carousel platform. Outside figures are more decorated than inside figures because they are the most visible, and so are generally more sought after than their plainer inside brethren. Standers are the most common position in which animals were made; prancing and leaping are less often seen. Park paint vs. resurfaced or repainted figures are also important areas where desirability is determined.

Generally, a carousel figure retaining its weathered, original surface or as close to it as possible (called "park paint") is more desirable than a figure that has been stripped and over-restored (for the distinction between 'conservation' and 'restoration,' see page 103).

The world auction record for a single carousel figure is $174,900, set in 1992 for *Bruno*, a St. Bernard manufactured by the Philadelphia Toboggan Company and sold by Gordon Riewe Auction Associates, Lapeer, Michigan. The second highest price paid for a carousel figure at auction is $148,000, paid in 1989 for a circa-1900 Dentzel rooster (Philadelphia Toboggan Company bought Dentzel in the early twentieth century). Otherwise, the range of prices for good and better commonly available carousel standers is anywhere from $15,000–50,000.

Decoys

A given record may remain static for years and then shift dramatically several times in a short period. Such is the case with American waterfowl decoys.

In July 1986, collector Russell Aitken set the record for an American decoy when he bought a circa-1915 preening pintail by A. Elmer Crowell of East Harwich, Massachusetts, for $319,000 at R. W. Oliver's, Kennebunk, Maine. That record held for 11 years. In January 2000, Sotheby's New York sold the decoy collection of Dr. James M. McCleery, a noted waterfowl decoy collector, during which, a circa-1917 sleeping Canada goose, also by A. Elmer Crowell, sold for $684,500, a new auction record for an American waterfowl decoy. In January 2003, following Russell Aitken's death, his decoy collection was sold at Christie's New York. Once again, the Crowell pintail that set the record in 1986 reasserted itself as the alpha decoy when it sold to a dealer on behalf of a private collector for $801,500.

To provide some perspective on this market, it should be noted that most American waterfowl decoys sell for a fractional percentage of these figures. Among the criteria decoy collectors review are whether or not the decoy can be attributed to a known maker. As with other areas of the American folk art marketplace, some makers enjoy greater demand and higher prices than others. It is also important whether or not the decoy was used and, if so, in what capacity, and how original or not its surface remains. For decoys where none of those questions can be conclusively answered (or the answers are "unknown, decorative, and repainted," in that order) the market for waterfowl decoys is a few hundred dollars, not more than $1,000, unless there is something unusual or attributable about the bird. Note: The same cannot necessarily be said for miniature bird carvings which are a related but separate market from waterfowl decoys.

Weathervanes

Weathervanes are among the most popular American folk art forms to collect. Some purists take exception to weathervanes because they are often factory-made objects rather than those produced by individuals. While the highest price paid at auction for an American weathervane is a record that will probably hold for some time, the standing for second-highest price paid to fourth-highest price paid is a constantly shifting battle with winners quickly supplanted by the next contender.

The world auction record for any American weathervane was set in January 1990 with the Sotheby's New York sale of property from the collection of Bernard Barenholtz. As was widely reported in the press at the time, Stephen Score, a Boston antiques dealer, bought the majestic and highly abstracted horse with rider stamped by its maker, J. Howard & Co., for $770,000.

The second-highest price at auction for an American weathervane was more recently set in November 2003 by Northeast Auctions, a major Portsmouth, New Hampshire, firm specializing in Americana, Maritime, and China Trade art. Ron Bourgeault, Northeast Auction's founder and principal auctioneer, sold the pristine weathervane of an Indian shooting an arrow to a private collector for $365,500, a formidable sum that is nonetheless still less than half the record. The weathervane had graced the cover of a June 1984 Sotheby's New York sale, where it sold for $41,800, a price that, by 1984 standards, that was notable as well.

Less than two years earlier, the third-highest priced weathervane at auction had been the second. A rare L. W. Cushing & Son weathervane in the form of a squirrel clutching a nut, whose surface was untouched beyond a white compound filling bullet holes the squirrel acquired during its later life as a target, sold for $292,000 at Christie's New York in January 2002. Stephen Score, the Boston dealer who set the record price for a weathervane in 1990, also purchased this weathervane.

Following the realignment of weathervane auction records after Northeast Auction's Indian Shooting Arrow, a copper locomotive weathervane sold at Skinner, Inc., in June 2002 for $237,000, became the fourth-highest-priced weathervane to sell at auction. The buyer was a collector. Fifteen years earlier, in March 1987, Skinner sold a similar locomotive weathervane for $203,500, suggesting both the relative rarity and desirability for certain examples of this type of weathervane.

A few factors should be noted regarding several of these high weathervane price results. First, regarding the results in excess of $200,000 for the two locomotive forms, both prices occurred during markets that generally witnessed very competitive results for rare and desirable offerings (i.e. best); lesser objects, at least in the later 2003 market, struggled more frequently at auction than during the superheated art market of the 1980s. Second, with respect to the price results on the Indian Shooting Arrow weathervane at Northeast Auctions in November 2003, the same buyer of that weathervane was rumored to have purchased the locomotive at Skinner, Inc. in June 2002. Accordingly, these price results may also reflect the manner in which one active collector seeking the best example of a certain form can drive a market to levels it might not have otherwise achieved. To provide counterpoint prices to the highest end of the weathervane market, good examples of common forms, such as a running horse, can be found at auction for $10,000–15,000. Depending on the auction, such as a sale in which a large quantity of weathervanes is included, such forms may even be found for between $5,000–10,000.

Textiles
Needlework

The record for the highest price paid at auction for an example of American needlework is the Hannah Otis canvas work chimneypiece. Showing a view of Boston, the large eighteenth-century needlework sold for $1,157,500 at Sotheby's New York in January 1996 to the Museum of Fine Arts, Boston.

Boston "Fishing Lady" pictures, as they are called, reign where second- and third-highest auction prices for American needlework are concerned as well. Second-place honors at auction go to another canvas work picture also made in the Boston area during the second quarter of the eighteenth century. The anonymously done work was sold at Butterfield's San Francisco in June 2003 for $611,500 to a needlework dealer. Only a month before, the third-highest-priced needlework at auction had been the second. This third Boston Fishing Lady scene, also done anonymously, circa 1750, and which remained in its original double-arched frame, sold to a private collector for $467,200 at Sotheby's New York in May 2003. By the time this book is published, these records may have changed again!

Prices for eighteenth-century needleworks rapidly descend from these lofty heights. Several have sold between $200,000–300,000. A few more have sold between $100,000–200,000, and the majority have sold for much less. Depending on the nature of the form, how it was originally used, and in what condition it survives, these eighteenth-century American needleworks have sold for as little as $28,000 (Christie's, June 1993, lot 96) and even less. Given that well-to-do young girls in eighteenth-century England were taught similar needlework skills, among the critical factors in determining value for these forms is conclusively confirming that the work is American. A viable history of ownership in America combined with a specific aesthetic relationship to other similar documented American needleworks is usually what collectors seek in establishing the identity of one of these works. Similarly, wrought wool tent-stitched pictures made in England at the same period, usually showing an Old Testament scene, generally sell at a fraction of the low end of the market for an American work.

Quilts

Quilts are probably one of the easiest areas of the American folk art marketplace to understand: Everyone, at one time or another, has needed to stay warm. Whether pieced, appliquéd, stuffed, or stenciled, the quilter's art satisfies this need creatively and often beautifully. Feminist historians would further observe that, at a time when women had little or no public voice, left equally as little (if not less) documentation of themselves and had few legal rights, quilts also provided a political and social pulpit from which to express their views. While many quilts chronicled life's events and celebrated the bonds of community and family, some went even further. Quilts memorialized war heroes, such as Major Ringgold, a Maryland officer killed in the Mexican War but remembered in a discernible group of Baltimore Album quilts; promoted the Temperance Movement; raised money for veterans of the Civil War; and even endorsed political candidates (Abraham Lincoln's beginnings in a log cabin were the inspiration for the Log Cabin quilt pattern). Today, in the case of Amish quilts currently made for use outside the sect, quilt making preserves a specific culture and way of life.

It should be no surprise, then, that the highest price at auction for an American quilt went to an object created during one of the most important events in this nation's history. The "Reconciliation Quilt," as it has become known, was made by Lucinda Ward Honstain of Brooklyn, New York, circa 1867, to express abolitionist support and the hope for a stronger United States following the horror of the Civil War. Forty distinct pictorial squares comprise the quilt and show scenes of domestic, commercial, and political life during the ante- and postbellum United States. One of the squares portrays an emancipated African-American man with the inscription "Master I Am Free"; another features the embroidered date *Nov. 18, 1867*, which was the year African-Americans gained the right to vote. With other blocks depicting additional scenes, including Jefferson Davis's release from prison, the quilt has come to embody the wish for reconciliation between North and South. Sold at Sotheby's New York in 1991 for $264,000, the quilt was donated by its subsequent owners, collectors Robert and Ardis James, to the University of Nebraska's International Quilt Study Center in January 2002.

Other high prices for quilt forms have tended to go to album quilt forms as well. A Baltimore Album quilt attributed to nineteenth-century Marylander Mary Updegraff from the Collection of Sam and Nancy Starr sold at Christie's New York in January 1989 for $189,000. More recently, in November 2003, another Civil War–era album quilt brought $130,000 at auction at Skinner, Inc., in Boston, Massachusetts. While these last two prices are not records, they nonetheless show how rare examples of American folk art that document important national events can bring strong prices at auction. In April 2004, a rare stenciled bedcover sold at Gould Auctioneers, Gardiner, Maine, to a dealer buying for a private collector for $231,000.

With the influx of easy-to-care-for reproduction quilts made in traditional patterns, the majority of the American antique quilt market has become quite modest. Antique quilts are fragile, susceptible to damage, and hard to display. With the majority of buyers interested in quilts more for the look than the object, many prefer an inexpensive reproduction that accomplishes the same effect and can be thrown in the washing machine rather than paying a few hundred dollars for a high-maintenance textile. Prices range anywhere from the low $20,000s to $50,000s for "better" antique quilts and are usually purchased by more serious collectors and dealers. Good examples can bring as little as a few hundred dollars to under $5,000 at auction.

School Girl Art

While Boston Fishing Ladies and silk needlework pictures were the educational mainstay for well-to-do American girls in the eighteenth-century Boston and Philadelphia areas, aesthetic mores had changed what young girls were taught by the time the United States celebrated its first quarter century. Combinations of media—watercolor pigment on silk ground, sometimes with metallic foil appliqués, needlework, pen work (usually done by the teacher), or all three, and often referencing a Classical theme, in addition to Biblical stories, were the fashionable curricula in the years following the War of 1812. While the category of School Girl Art encompasses other forms, silk pictures are usually the most colorful and graphic of all.

The highest price paid at auction for an example of American School Girl Art is $374,000 for a watercolor and gold foil on silk picture of *Aurora*, probably done in an as yet unidentified Massachusetts school between 1818 and 1822. It was sold to a private collector at Christie's New York in June 1989.

Painting
On Canvas

It is only appropriate that the most iconic image in American folk art, Edward Hicks's *Peaceable Kingdom*, is also the work for which the all-time highest price for any example of American folk art was ever paid at auction. This occurred at Christie's New York in January 1999 when a *Peaceable Kingdom* sold for $4,732,500 to a dealer, rivaling even in its auction price some works by Impressionist artists. Since Hicks's is such an unusual case study, however, this look at record auction prices in the marketplace for American folk art paintings will include other works on canvas besides those by Hicks.

Edward Hicks was an itinerant Quaker minister who created, between 1825 and 1849, more than sixty oil on canvas versions of the Prophecy of Isaiah in which the wolf and lamb, the leopard and kid, the calf, lion, and fatling, peacefully coexist (Isaiah 11:6–9). The painting is an allegory of hope for a secular world that human adversaries might also live in harmony. To the extent that Hicks was explicitly referring to schismatic events within his own Quaker community during the time in which he painted these works, his message transcends those circumstances and resonates today. Trained as a coach and sign painter when not pursuing his traveling ministry, Hicks painted other subjects as well, some of which touch on themes similar to the *Peaceable Kingdom* series. Some of these are memory paintings from his childhood or were impor-tant historical scenes, such as the signing of the Declaration of Independence and Washington Crossing the Delaware. Of all of Hicks's painted subjects, however, the *Peaceable Kingdom* series is the most popular in today's marketplace, with most known versions in museum collections.

The second-highest price ever paid at auction for an example of American folk art is also by Edward Hicks and is one of his memory paintings. Completed circa 1845, toward the end of Hicks's life, and showing the farm in

Bucks County, Pennsylvania, owned by David Twining (where Hicks was sent to live as a twelve-year-old child following his mother's death), the canvas had never left the family for whom Hicks had painted it. The work was one of four known scenes of Twining's farm, two others of which are in museum collections. Sold in the same January 1999 sale that witnessed a *Peaceable Kingdom* establish the auction record for any work of American folk art, *The Residence of David Twining, 1785*, sold for $1,432,500 to a private collector.

Although Edward Hicks set the two top prices for American folk art, it would be a mistake to extrapolate from this that all works by Edward Hicks bring big money. To the contrary, although Hicks's *Peaceable Kingdoms* have brought heady prices, there is a world of difference between a $4.7M canvas and a $1.4M canvas, and that difference is more than just the under bidder. All other subjects by Hicks take second seat to his kingdoms, with prices for these works generally ranging from $300,000–600,000. A third painting by Edward Hicks in the same January 1999 Christie's New York sale, a highly unusual occurrence in and of itself, *Jonathan and David at the Stone Ezel* sold for $70,700. Hicks's market is subject driven, not artist driven. Beyond two specific subjects painted by Edward Hicks, some of the highest prices paid at auction for American folk paintings have otherwise been paid for folk portraits.

Portraiture was the most popular form of painting in its day. During the early collecting years of 1920–1950, portraits were almost as popular to collect as they had been to commission in the first place. Changing tastes and collecting mores, however, have somewhat diminished the allure of this once vital cornerstone of the American folk art market, such that collectors are much more discriminating in their portrait collecting. Most American folk art portraits can be obtained for less than $10,000; many can even be had for less than $5,000 at auction. Some of the most important known itinerant artists, such as Ammi Phillips and Erastus Salisbury Field, can be acquired at these levels, though slightly better examples of their work and others are in the $15,000–30,000 range.

Nonetheless, works by a few acknowledged masters of the American itinerant tradition have achieved staggering results. A double portrait of *Comfort Starr Mygatt and his daughter Lucy Mygatt (Adams)* by deaf mute itinerant artist John Brewster Jr., sold to a dealer at Sotheby's New York, January 1988, for the record price of $852,500. That record remained unapproached until November 2001, when a double portrait by Sheldon Peck, *Mr. and Mrs. William Vaughan of Aurora, Illinois*, came to auction at Sotheby's New York and sold for $830,750 to a dealer on behalf of a private collector.

The record for the third-highest price paid at auction is a case study in relative values and oversaturation of the market. In 1984, a portrait of a little girl in a red dress with a dog by her side painted by the known itinerant artist, Ammi Phillips, was consigned to auction. It created headlines a few months later in January 1985 when it sold at Christie's New York for $682,000, an auction record not only for the artist but, at that time, for an American folk portrait as well (*Comfort Starr Mygatt and his daughter . . .* would not come up for auction for another three years). The painting was even adapted by the United States Postal Service as a stamp. On the basis of that sale result, works by Ammi Phillips suddenly found their way to the auction block with greater regularity. Research published in 1968 on Ammi Phillips showed that the artist was prolific; consignments following the sale of *Girl in a Red Dress* showed that Phillips's work was even more abundant than had heretofore been imagined. By October 1992, the American folk art marketplace had become so overstocked with portraits by Ammi Phillips that a single portrait of a man in relatively good condition and estimated conservatively at $4,000–6,000 found no interest among auction bidders. While an unknown single man tends to be one of the least desirable types of American folk portraits to collect (and so the hardest to sell!) and October 1992 was the bottom of the art market recession of the early 1990s, the gulf between $682,000 and not even $4,000 is nonetheless considerable indeed.

The fourth-highest price at auction for American folk painting is also a double portrait by Sheldon Peck of *Frances Almira Millener and Fanny Root Millener* descended to the great-grandchildren of Fanny Root Millener before it was acquired and then deaccessioned by the Cayuga Museum, with the proceeds to benefit the museum. The painting sold for $647,500 to a collector at Christie's New York in January 20003. While the accomplishment of two paintings in the top four highest prices paid at auction for an American folk art portrait going to the same artist may lead some to conclude "$600,000–800,000 is what Sheldon Pecks are worth," in fact, the majority of Peck's work generally sells for under $100,000, with most examples well under that price point.

On Furniture

Painting also appears on wood in the form of paint-decorated furniture. The highest price paid at auction for an example of such furniture occurred in May 1995 during the sale of the Collection of Dr. Henry P. Deyerle, conducted by Sotheby's on-site in Charlottesville, Virginia. A blanket chest by Shenandoah (now Page) County, Virginia, German-American artist Johannes Spitler (1774–1837) brought $343,500 and was bought by Colonial Williamsburg.

Game Boards

Painted game boards have become an increasingly active area of the American folk art marketplace over the last five years in part because there is crossover collecting competition from the Toys, Dolls, and Games marketplace, and in part because it is almost impossible to tell an American example from a non-American one without some extenuating evidence, such as original paint showing an American flag. Nevertheless, some hefty prices have been realized for these forms.

The auction record for an American decorated game board is tied between two sales, almost six months apart from one another. The record was first set in August 2000 at Northeast Auctions' sale of the collection of Virginia Cave, where a painted game board decorated with American flags sold for $46,000. The game board had been in the collection of the Art Institute of Chicago, which deaccessioned the object through Sotheby's New York in January 1997. During that sale, the patriotic form sold for $25,300; while the specifics of its second sale are unknown, it is nonetheless an impressive indicator of that market's growth that within four years the price had almost doubled for the same object. Almost six months later, in February 2001 at Skinner, Inc., then in Bolton, Massachusetts, a second paint-decorated game board brought the same price: 46,000. The second example was a folding Parcheesi board, also part of a well-marketed single-owner sale (The Collection of Peter Brams), and sold to a Massachusetts collector.

Outsider Art

Several artists in this oeuvre have achieved notable prices. In contrast to the rest of American folk art, in which prices are often strongest in or near where the object was made, strong prices for outsider art have been more consistently fetched in Europe rather than at auction in the United States. The following list consists of only a few of the artists whose works have been highly sought after on the auction block.

The top price for a work by **Martin Ramirez** (1885–1960), the twentieth-century Mexican-born paranoid schizophrenic artist who began drawing in the 1950s while institutionalized, was set in January 2003 with the sale of Robert Greenberg's collection at Christie's New York. The drawing, titled *Alamentosa* and painted circa 1953, sold for $95,600 to a South American buyer.

William Edmondson (1870–1951) was an African-American who grew up in Nashville, Tennessee, and worked in a variety of manual labor jobs before having a vision from God later in life that his purpose was to make sculpture. Using found materials—limestone from demolished houses and road projects and "chisels" made from railroad spikes, the 60-year-old Edmondson began to make crudely fashioned angels and Biblical characters as well as figures of animals and popular personalities of his day. His first projects were tombstones for the local African-American community. Despite his humble beginnings, Edmondson was the first African-American artist to have a one-man show at the Museum of Modern Art in 1937 (in part because of Holger Cahill and Dorothy Miller) and was more recently part of a retrospective hosted by the Cheekwood Museum, the largest institutional repository of Edmondson's work. While John Ollman of Fleisher/Ollman Gallery claimed in a press interview surrounding the Greenberg auction (which included an important example of Edmondson's work that subsequently failed to sell), that $305,000 is the highest price paid for a work by Edmondson, the highest auction price—an important distinction—was actually paid for *Birdbath*, a 1940s limestone sculpture which sold at Sotheby's New York in October 2000 for $236,750 to a representative for a private collector.

Bill Traylor (c. 1856–1949), an African-American artist born into slavery, was a factory worker and homeless welfare recipient in Montgomery, Alabama, before he created his vivid menagerie of colorful works on paper between 1939 and 1942. Discovered by another artist, Charles Shannon, who subsequently supplied Traylor with most of his materials, Traylor's work depicts men and women, animals (some of them based on fantasy), and shapes juxtaposed against each other or in isolation, but always caught in a kinetic moment. Charles Shannon documented Traylor's work, preserved it, and spearheaded Traylor exhibitions both in Alabama and at New York City's Museum of Modern Art in 1941. After 1942, Traylor produced comparatively few works. He died in a nursing home in 1949. Through Shannon's documentation, we know that Traylor created approximately 1,800 of his wildly graphic "snapshots," and Traylor's work remains among the icons of the Outsider Art tradition.

Man with Yoke, a pencil and gouache on cardboard image that had been owned by Charles Shannon, brought the record auction price for a work by Bill Traylor. Estimated at $175,000–225,000, it sold to a collector for $203,750 at Sotheby's New York in January 2001.

Born on St. Helena, a coastal island off South Carolina, **Sam Doyle** (1906–1985) portrayed scenes of life on the island as well as fictional events and the popular figures of his day. Doyle completed the ninth grade in school, after which he worked in a variety of unskilled labor jobs on St. Helena and nearby Parris Island. Doyle began to paint in the mid-1940s, like Traylor and Edmondson, using materials that were easily available to him—roofing tin and enamel house paint. Doyle's paintings are characterized by a bold and liberal use of paint with scenes and personalities occupying a larger-than-life space on whatever surface he chose to use.

In May 2003 Slotin Folk Art, an auction company located in Buford, Georgia, and dedicated to championing self-taught artists, featured *Larry Rivers, Harlem Globe Troter* [sic], a house painting on roofing tin work in which the athlete spins a basketball on his finger. The painting had an impressive provenance as well—it had been exhibited at The High Museum of Art in Atlanta, Georgia, and had been in the collection of well-known American folk art collectors/authors Chuck and Jan Rosenak. The painting established a record price at auction for Doyle when it sold for $49,500. ◾

6

THINK AND TALK LIKE AN EXPERT

After you have done some initial study to learn about what you like and its variety of appearance, the most important key to collecting is to buy what you like. Entering the marketplace with a financial investment agenda is as risky and fraught with failure as any other 'get rich quick' scheme. There is no way to predict what will be valuable next year or in ten years. Collecting objects that enrich your daily experience and make you smile will always weather any changes in marketplace value. Collecting those objects to which you respond is also more motivating for further inquiry, study, and learning.

What to Collect

Having identified the one kind of object or group of objects that sparks your interest, the next two rules of collecting are to buy the best that you can afford and to know your collection for what it is. It is better to spend a higher amount (that is still within your budget!) for an object that meets a greater number of your collecting criteria than to go for that bargain-priced object that meets none of your qualifications but sure looks great. Not only will the former strategy result in a more consistent quality level within your collection, but, oftentimes, if an object is too good to be true, it probably is too good to be true. Further, it is acceptable to buy an object that doesn't meet every collectibility criterion so long as you understand how those omissions affect value. You also have to know that what the object isn't should affect what you pay for it, and that these same factors will probably affect value in the future as well. Buying the best you can afford and being realistic about your collection relate directly to condition.

Condition: The Key Element to Determine Desirability

In collecting American folk art, condition refers to two factors.

First, condition refers to the degree to which the object retains the original elements or decoration of its maker without any alteration, restoration, or 'help' from a later hand. Those objects that survive entirely unaltered from their original state are called 'pristine.' Though these may appear faded and abused, that's because they are untouched from the day they were made!

Train yourself to question whether the object's manufacture and use make sense for its present appearance. Comparatively few objects do, in fact, survive in pristine condition; many, however, survive in near-pristine or very acceptable shape. The issue for you is to determine how many degrees from perfect your object of desire is and what that means to you in terms of value.

Second, condition refers to what has happened to an object when it has been altered from its original appearance. What are the levels of acceptable repair or restoration for something that is not pristine? For example, all other criteria being equal, a portrait on canvas with a repaired and inpainted tear in the background may be acceptable; a similar portrait with a repaired and inpainted tear to the face of its sitter probably is not. In the case of the latter, the very purpose of the work—the likeness of the sitter's face—has been compromised. Whether or not that repair leaves the painting in desirable or undesirable condition depends on a variety of factors including the overall quality of the painting, whether or not the artist or sitter is known, and how many other similar works in better condition might be available. From a condition perspective, the desirability of the painting also highlights the difference between conservation and restoration and important nuances within those definitions.

Conservation and Restoration Guidelines

There is an important distinction between 'conservation' and 'restoration.' 'Conservation' attempts to halt or slow whatever natural degradation or aging process is already in play to preserve the object. Present conservation standards dictate that any work done to an object should be reversible or easy to undo. 'Restoration' attempts to bring the object back to its original appearance at the time of its manufacture and is usually not reversible. Generally, from a market perspective, conservation is desirable while restoration is not. The logic behind this distinction is twofold: first, given the reversibility of conservation and irreversibility of restoration, it is better to keep the option open that the work can be undone— who knows what the next owner will want. Doing something irreversible may lessen value; and who knows what the next generation will discover! Second, we, in the twenty-first century, cannot possibly know how an historical object looked at its creation, so to restore an object is to impose an idea of its original appearance, which is usually conjectural. As with everything in American folk art, however, there are exceptions to the rule, and bad conservation is worse than good restoration.

Where conservation and restoration are concerned, it is important to understand the time and circumstances in which the object was altered. During the 1950s and

1960s, the acceptable conservation technique that addressed cupping and flaking for most oil on canvas paintings was to 'wax reline' the work. A thin layer of wax was placed between a new canvas and the aging, degrading canvas whose paint was flaking off. This wax "sandwich" was then heat sealed, adhering the new canvas to the old and allowing the wax to seep through the old canvas, effectively binding the pigment to the new canvas in much the same way an iron-on decal works. While the positive result was that the canvas was reinforced, its brittle paint no longer flaked off the picture, and the overall subject was preserved, the negative result was that any depth of pigment created by the artist as part of the work was flattened and the process is not feasibly reversible. Even if one were to undertake the painstaking and expensive work to undo this process, the end result inherently would still never be what the painting was prior to the pressure-heat treatment of wax relining.

Conversely, numerous examples exist in which an object whose form is well known and well documented turns up missing an original part, such as the feet on a blanket chest. In such instances where the missing part can be researched for historical accuracy and its replacement or reattachment fully documented for any future owner, restoration bears very positive results. Both circumstances should be taken into account in assessing value.

Essential Tools of Collecting

For a listing of where to obtain these tools, see "Supplies" in the Resource Guide.

Black Light

Among the most commonly seen tools of the trade is a combination short wave–long wave ultraviolet light called a "black light." While the long wave light emitted is actually purple and should not be looked at directly, it can be used to determine changes in a variety of surfaces because different compounds fluoresce differently under ultraviolet stimulation. An object may appear uniform to the naked eye but be an entirely different story under the black light.

The key to using a black light effectively is to know what the object in question is and is not supposed to do under the light, to know how different materials fluoresce, and to know what the question is that the black light will address. The presence of dark black areas or differing fluorescence on certain media does not automatically mean repair or replacement. Further, there is frequently a misperception with black lights that they will answer every question about an object and can determine authenticity. On the contrary, like any tool, a black light can only address, to a limited extent, the purpose for which it was intended. If an object were made with the intention to deceive and, for example, old paints were applied with old tools and aged accordingly, a black light will not reveal the forgery.

Black lights are used to examine works on paper, ceramics, and painted objects. On paper, a black light can detect repaired tears and ended-out losses; on ceramics, a black light can reveal repaired cracks, replaced losses and reglazed surfaces; on paintings, a black light may show inpainting and a re-varnished, or screening varnished, canvas. While a black light cannot penetrate an excessive or screening varnish, one can extrapolate from its presence that there is something to screen—this isn't always the case, but is a good example of healthy skepticism where condition is concerned. Remember that certain compounds, such as metallic pigments (gilding), are supposed to fluoresce black; and a black light does not determine the age of a work of art, merely differences in surface or body compounds.

A variety of different black lights are available to consumers. Most small, lightweight, portable black lights are not worth the investment; the more bulky, powerful models requiring an electrical outlet are.

Cloth tape measure

A tape measure calibrated in inches and in metric measurements helps to determine if an object is out of round (calipers can be used for smaller turned objects) and how an object's dimensions relate to others of its type. Knowing the typical dimensions of the material category into which your object falls is important in determining its authenticity. Most chairs are approximately 17 inches high from the floor to the seat frame. A significant departure from that standard requires an explanation (If too tall, are there casters on the chair that are not original? If too short, was the chair cut down?). If an artist or school always produces works within a given range of dimensions and the object you are examining doesn't meet those size guidelines, what does that mean? Likewise, if a round-top table purports to be eighteenth-century, but has a fully round top, you have a problem. Wood shrinks across the grain, so the dimensions of that top should be a little smaller perpendicular to the grain than parallel to it. Cloth is the preferred material for tape measures because it will not cut, mark, scrape, or mar the object you are examining.

Magnifying glass with light

A 5X magnifying lens with a built-in light source is invaluable for examining more delicate objects with finer detail such as needlework, works on paper, and even the grain on a limb of furniture. This tool is also effective for examining and understanding specific elements of an object such as a solder repair on a piece of metal or restored decoration on a painted surface.

10X loupe

For the closest examination of fine work, a jeweler's, or 10X, loupe shows the greatest detail. Using a loupe requires a little practice. The reward in seeing either the most delicate repair work or the finest original work is well worth it.

Flat head screwdriver

This essential tool can be used on furniture and with paintings. Whether determining the originality of a top to its base or gathering evidence toward the probable date of manufacture of a piece of furniture by examining how its original hardware was fabricated, a flat head screwdriver can provide essential information. Likewise, carefully removing the frame from a painting can reveal that a painting has been cut down or can confirm that a painting has been restretched, relined, or is otherwise not on its original support.

Portable light source

Careful examination with a powerful light source, such as a portable halogen bike light, a scuba flashlight or, not so portable, a photo lamp (requires an outlet), can reveal repairs, surface and color inconsistencies, or replacements not otherwise visible to the naked eye.

Analyzing the Marketplace: Where and How to Buy and Sell

The marketplace offers a variety of ways to buy and sell antiques. The most common are at a flea market or antiques show, through an individual dealer or auction house and, more recently and commonly, on the Internet.

Three important rules attend buying:

First and most important: Know your source. Whether the descendant of an original owner, an individual dealer at a flea market, antiques show or in their shop, an auction house, or an online seller, a credible source is willing to guarantee the object and provide recourse to you, the buyer, should you discover the object is not what you thought it was. Should you become a seller, be prepared to do the same. A written description at the time of sale will often settle any confusion about the nature of the object; likewise, a written return policy/money-back guarantee is valuable protection. In most cases when dealing with a reputable seller, these issues will not come into play.

Second, when dealing with any seller, particularly an auction house, be sure you understand the terms of sale and glossary that relates to a sale: a "Federal Table" and a "Federal Style Table" are two very different creatures; likewise, degrees of separation between authentic and copy exist when artists are concerned as well. Is a work "by" the artist, "attributed or ascribed to" the artist, "school of" the artist, or "in the manner of" the artist? Usually each distinction brings you an additional step away from an original work by a given artist. While the Internet is a means of selling antiques, this is an especially high-risk venue: Unlike a national chain that sells thousands of the same item, there is no standard or quality control in the sale of antiques; each object is unique, and often impossible to inspect physically. You also don't always know from whom you are buying.

Finally, unless you know the seller or are comfortable with the risks of buying on the Internet, always examine the object in person before purchase or have a clear right of refusal upon examination agreement before money changes hands.

Price and rarity aside, it's a buyer's marketplace when it comes to taking your time, figuring out who has what, and establishing a relationship with a reputable source. For newer collectors, it may be worthwhile to seek the advice of a reputable consultant, a "hired gun" who can walk you through the vetting and buying process.

Similarly, these rules can be applied to selling as well. Just as buying can be costly, selling can be as well. Depending on the venue of sale, a variety of fees, including a commission to the agent through whom you sell, can apply.

If selling through a dealer, the dealer might make an acceptable offer to buy the object outright or may take it on consignment, in which case the fee may be a percentage of the mutually agreed upon sale price. These are both areas in which knowledge of the value of your property will serve you well; if you don't have that yet, an outside opinion would be in both parties' interests since establishing a commission on the basis of value can lead if not to a conflict of interest, the possible perception of it. In either scenario, a clearly written agreement, including a receipt for any property sold or consigned, should be part of the arrangement.

If selling through an auction house, again, a number of fees may apply. As a general rule, the larger the auction house, the greater the number of selling charges. These can include fees for illustrating the property in a glossy, published catalog; insurance fees (this is common to many auction houses regardless of size); transportation costs for getting your property to the auction; and a lesser "unsold" fee designed to recompense the auction house for the costs of sale it incurred even if your property didn't sell (staff hours preparing a sale, advertising costs, overhead, and insurance, among other things; selling is expensive for the auction houses as well). While it used to be that the size of the auction house also had bearing on the successful exposure of a consignment to relevant buyers, the Internet is changing this old truism. In 2002 alone, several small auction houses that posted

their property for sale on their Web sites set formidable prices.[10]

Whichever route you choose, pick one or the other, not both. The phrase "shopped" refers to property that sellers have offered to one or more vendors in a limited amount of time, thus overexposing the property to the marketplace. Generally, buyers are interested in property that has not lingered too long for sale and has not been passed from owner to owner in a brief time period. The more venues in which you offer a work of art, the more you risk devaluing your own property. Once you have committed to a sale and to a vendor, let them do the marketing and selling.

As with anything involving the art market, there is always risk that your property won't sell. Be realistic about value, regardless of what you paid for it. If your property doesn't sell, you still have something you liked enough to take home with you; the best course of action is to take it home again and live with it a little longer.

Cast-Iron Weathervane of a Prancing Horse with Sheet Iron Tail
c. 1880, Rochester Iron Works, New Hampshire. Approximately 38" L
Photo courtesy David Wheatcroft Antiques; Private collection

[10] 25 May 2002 Stair Galleries, Hudson, New York, set an auction record of $67,500 for a watercolor landscape by Wisconsin folk artist Paul Seifert. In June 2002 Mike Clum Auctions of Rushville, Ohio, achieved several notable prices for property in the final sale of Clark and Mary Garrett's estate.

Fakes and Forgeries

Frauds exist in any area of the marketplace where there is money to be made and a buyer willing to believe. Almost every collection contains a fake or two or more, and every collector/dealer/curator/auction house specialist makes a mistake. If an object is made with the intent to deceive, chances are it will fool at least one or more people. Although the following directly contradicts the American way, one guideline to follow that may prevent such costly errors is "Guilty until proven innocent." As you examine the object, make it prove itself to you; consider why every detail of its appearance, construction, and decoration makes sense for what it purports to be.

While every buyer wants to avoid fakes, spurious material is a good learning opportunity. Many larger museums such as the Winterthur and the Metropolitan Museum of Art's American Wing keep a "Study Collection" of forgeries whose subtleties teach us the faker's art. Learning what's wrong about an object can be as valuable and as important as learning what is right about it.

Several notable areas of forgery have entered the marketplace over the last 25 years. The best known among these is scrimshaw. The majority of forgeries are molded polymers designed, to varying degrees of credibility, to look like a decorated whale tooth. Early in plastic "scrimshaw" production, buyers were advised to be aware by means of "the hot pin test": a pin was warmed and its point pressed into the so-called tooth body. If the pin did not penetrate the surface, the tooth was real; if it did, the tooth was fake. Forgery has evolved like everything else, and fakers subsequently made heat-resistant polymers that defied the hot pin test, so scrimshaw buyers must go back to learning the difference in color and feel of the real versus the deception.

During the height of the American quilt market in the 1980s, another forgery niche was for Amish crib quilts. Although the quilt market has subsequently declined dramatically, those new crib quilts made in the style of original Amish work are still out there and buyers must be aware of them.

Among the most enduring areas of the American folk art market is the demand for American weathervanes. As a

Tavern Sign: Wingate's Tavern
Dated 1814, New England. Carved and painted wood with iron mounts, double sided. Approximately 5' H × 3' W Photo courtesy Sotheby's; Private collection

result, the quantity of forged and/or heavily restored weathervanes on the market has reached glut proportions. Myrna Kaye's two-part series in *Maine Antique Digest* (May 2002, pp. 40–41D; October 2002, p. 7C) identified a group of old and real weathervane molds used in recent production. While making "new old" weathervanes is one area of forgery, resurfacing and/or heavily restoring damaged weathervanes has also become lucrative in the face of increasingly high prices paid for these sculptural forms. Again, if you are buying, the caveat is to know your source.

Other sculpture for which there has been an established forgery market—ever since well-known collectors like Henry Francis du Pont and Electra Havemeyer Webb began paying high prices for certain forms—include that of Pennsylvania German woodworker Wilhelm Schimmel. More recently, the explosion in the market for Pennsylvania German folk art beyond that state's borders has witnessed a rise in spurious examples of fraktur and carving among other well-publicized examples.

Conclusion

Armed with the critical thinking and healthy skepticism of a seasoned collector, you need the ability to understand what you are seeing and the vocabulary to communicate your concerns. By understanding collecting principles and using some tools for assistance, you are ready for some field work. Start attending flea markets and antiques shows to test and hone your skills as well as the ideas you have learned in this book. Join a collecting club or museum group to meet people with similar interests. Dealers and collectors are among the most generous in the world with their expertise. ◼

RESOURCE GUIDE

ASSOCIATIONS & ORGANIZATIONS

American Society of Appraisers
555 Herndon Parkway, Suite 125
Herndon, VA 20170
Phone: 703-478-2228
Fax: 703-742-8471
E-mail: asainfo@appraisers.org
Web site: www.appraisers.org

The Alliance for American Quilts
P. O. Box 6251
Louisville, KY 40206
Phone/Fax: 502-897-3819
E-mail: info@quiltalliance.org
Web site: www.quiltalliance.org

Appraisers Association of America
386 Park Avenue South, Suite 2000
New York, NY 10016
Phone: 212-889-5404
Fax: 212-889-5503
E-mail: aaa1@rcn.com
Web site: www.appraisersassoc.org

American Decorative Arts Forum of Northern California
California Legion of Honor
Lincoln Park
San Francisco, CA 94121
Phone: 415-431-6930
E-mail: info@adafca.org
Web site: www.adafca.org

The Folk Art Society in America
Box 17041
Richmond, VA 23226
Phone: 800-527-3655
E-mail: folkart@rmond.mind-spring.com
Web site: www.folkart.org

International Society of Appraisers
1131 SW 7th St., Suite 105
Renton, WA 98055
Phone: 206-241-0359
Fax: 206-241-0436
E-mail: isahq@isa-appraisers.org
Web site: www.isa-appraisers.org

AUCTION HOUSES

Many more auction houses exist in the United States than can realistically be included. However, the following list provides a geographically arranged selection of larger auction houses. Consulting the magazines and periodicals listed in this chapter, as well as your local newspaper, will also provide greater information for your area.

In addition to these live auction companies, eBay (www.ebay.com) and other on-line auction sites should also be routinely surveyed for offerings in American folk art.

Mid-Atlantic

Alderfer Auction Company
501 Fairgrounds Road
Hatfield, PA 19440
Phone: 215-393-3000
Fax: 215-368-9055
E-mail: info@alderferauction.com
Web site: www.alderferauction.com/home.asp

Bertoia Auctions
2141 DeMarco Drive
Vineland, NJ 08360
Phone: 856-692-1881
Fax: 856-692-8697
E-mail: Bill@BertoiaAuctions.com
Web site: www.bertoiaauctions.
com/index.html

Conestoga Auction Company, Inc.
768 Graystone Road
P. O. Box 1
Manheim, PA 17545
Phone: 717-898-7284
Fax: 717-898-6628
E-mail: ca@conestogaauction.com
Web site: www.conestogaauction.
com

Alex Cooper's Auctioneers, Inc
908 York Road
Towson, MD 21204
Phone: 410-828-4838 or
800-272-3145
Fax: 410-828-0875
E-mail: info@alexcooper.com
Web site: www.alexcooper.com/
antiqueAuctionsMain.html

Samuel T. Freeman & Co.
1808 Chestnut Street
Philadelphia, PA 19103
Phone: 215-563-9275
Fax: 215-563-8236
E-mail: Info@freemansauction.com
Web site: www.freemansauction.
com

Horst
50 Durlach Road
Ephrata, PA 17522
Phone: 717-738-3080
E-mail: sale@horstauction.com
Web site: www.horstauction.com

Richard Opfer Auctioneering, Inc.
1919 Greenspring Drive
Timonium, MD 21093
Phone: 410-252-5035
Fax: 410-252-5863
E-mail: info@opferauction.com
Web site: www.opferauction.com

Pook & Pook
P. O. Box 268
Downingtown, PA 19335
Phone: 610-269-4040 or
610-269-0695
Fax: 610-269-9274
E-mail: info@pookandpook.com
Web site: www.pookandpook.com

Sloan's & Kenyon
4605 Bradley Boulevard
Bethesda, MD 20815
Phone: 301-634-2330
Fax: 301-656-7074
E-mail:
info@sloansandkenyon.com
Web site: www.sloansandkenyon.
com

Weschler's
909 E Street, N.W.
Washington, D.C. 20004
Phone: local 202 -628- 1281;
national 800-331-1430
Fax: 202-628-2366
E-mail: fineart@weschlers.com
Web site: www.weschlers.com/
welcome.cfm

Midwest

Mike Clum Auctions Inc
7795 Cincinnati-Zanesville Rd. NE
Rushville, OH 43150
Phone: 740-536-7421 (Office)
740-536-9220 (Gallery)
Fax: 740-536-7242
E-mail: info@clum.com
Web site: www.clum.com

**Cowan's Historic Americana
Auctions**
673 Wilmer Avenue
Cincinnati, OH 45226
Phone: 513-871-1670
Fax: 513-871-8670
E-mail:
Info@HistoricAmericana.com
Web site: www.historicamericana.
com

Inlaid Box
Early twentieth century, found in New England. Wooden box inlaid with star and floral motifs and having hinged lid. 8"H × 6"W × 4"D
Private collection

Paint-decorated Washstand from a Suite of Cottage Furniture
Late nineteenth century, Pennsylvania. Original green and yellow polychrome finish. Approximately 48"H × 36"W
Private collection

DuMouchelle Art Galleries
409 East Jefferson Avenue
Detroit, MI 48226
Phone: 313-963-6255
Fax: 313-963-8199
E-mail: info@dumouchelle.com
Web site: www.dumouchelle.com

Garth's
2690 Stratford Road
P. O. Box 369
Delaware, OH 43015
Phone: 740-362-4771
Fax: 740-363-0164
E-mail: info@garths.com
Web site: www.garths.com

Leslie Hindman Inc
122 North Aberdeen Street
Chicago, IL 60607
Phone: 312-280-1212
Fax: 312-280-1211
Web site: www.lesliehindman.com

Ivey-Selkirk Auctioneers
7447 Forsyth Blvd.
St. Louis, MO 63105
Phone: 314-726-5515
Fax: 314-726-9908
E-mail: iveyselkirk@iveyselkirk.com
Web site: www.iveyselkirk.com

Neal Auction Co
4038 Magazine Street
New Orleans, LA 70115
Phone: local 504-899-5329; national
800-467-5329
Fax: 504-897-3808
E-mail: customerservice@
nealauction.com
Web site: www.nealauction.com/
indexie.html

Northeast

Christie's
20 Rockefeller Plaza
New York, NY 10020
Phone: 212-636-2000
Fax: 212-636-2399
Web site: www.christies.com

**Dawson & Nye Auctions &
Appraisals**
128 American Road
Morris Plains, NJ 07950
Phone: 973-984-6900
Fax: 973-984-6956
E-mail: info@dawsonandnye.com
Web site: www.dawsonandnye.com

Doyle New York
175 East 87th Street
New York, NY 10128
Phone: 212-427-2730
Fax: 212-369-0892
E-mail: info@DoyleNewYork.com
Web site: www.doylenewyork.com

Eldred's Auctioneers & Appraisers
1483 Route 6A
P. O. Box 796
East Dennis, MA   02641
Phone: 508-385-3116
Fax: 508-385-7201
E-mail: info@eldreds.com
Web site: www.eldreds.com

Guernsey's
108 East 73rd Street
New York, NY 10021
Phone: 212-794-2280
Fax: 212-744-3638
E-mail: auctions@guernseys.com
Web site: www.guernseys.com

**Guyette & Schmidt Inc.
(Waterfowl decoys)**
P. O. Box 522
West Farmington, ME 04992
Phone: 207-778-6256
Fax: 207-778-6501
E-mail:decoys@guyetteandschmidt.
com
Web site: www.guyetteandschmidt.
com

James D. Julia, Inc
P. O. Box 830
Fairfield, ME 04937
Phone: 207-453-7125
Fax: 207-453-2502
E-mail: jjulia@juliaauctions.com
Web site: www.juliaauctions.com

Northeast Auctions

93 Pleasant Street
Portsmouth, NH 03801
Phone: 603-433-8400
Fax: 603-433-0415
E-mail: contact@northeastauctions.
com
Web site: www.northeastauctions.
com

Rafael Osona Auctions

P. O. Box 2607
Nantucket, MA 02584
Phone: 508-228-3942
Fax: 508-228-8778
E-mail: osona@aol.com
Web site: www.rafaelosonaauction.
com

Skinner, Inc

The Heritage Online Garden
63 Park Plaza
Boston, MA 02116
Phone: 617-350-5400
Fax: 617-350-5429
E-mail: American@skinnerinc.
com
Web site: www.skinnerinc.com

Sotheby's

1334 York Ave
New York, NY 10021
Phone: 212-606-7000
Fax: 212-606-7107
Web site: http://search.sothebys.
com

Stair Galleries

33 Maple Ave.
P. O. Box 418
Claverack, NY 12513
Phone: 518-851-2544
Fax: 518-851-2558
E-mail: information@stairgalleries.
com
Web site: www.stairgalleries.com

Willis Henry

22 Main Street
Marshfield, MA 02050
Phone: 800-244-8466

Fax: 781-826-3520
E-mail: wha@willishenry.com
Web site: www.willishenry.com

Southeast

Ken Farmer Auctions

105 Harrison Street
Radford, VA 24141
Phone: 540-639-0939
Fax: 540-639-1759
E-mail: info@kfauctions.com
Web site: www.kenfarmer.com

Slotin Folk Art

Folk Fest, Inc.
5967 Blackberry Lane
Buford, GA 30518
Phone: 770-932-1000 or
404-403-4244
Fax: 770-932-0506
E-mail: folkfest@bellsouth.net
Web site: www.slotinfolkart.com/
index.html

Treasure Quest Auction Gallery

2581 Jupiter Park Dr., Suite E-9
Jupiter, FL 33458
Phone: local 561-741-0777; national
1-888-741-0777
E-mail: tqag@tqag.com
Web site: www.tqag.com

West

Auctions By The Bay, Inc.

2700 Saratoga Street
Alameda, CA 94501
Phone: 510-740-0220
Fax: 510-864-9198
E-mail: info@auctionsbythebay.com
Web site: www.auctionsbythebay.
com

Bonham & Butterfield's

220 San Bruno Avenue
San Francisco, CA 94103
Phone: 415-861-7500
Fax: 415-861-8951
E-mail: Info.US@bonhams.com
Web site: www.butterfields.com/
index.html

Coeur d'Alene Art Auction
P. O. Box 310
Hayden, ID 83835
Phone: 208-772-9009
Fax: 208-772-8294
E-mail: cdaartauction@
cdaartauction.com
Web site: www.cdaartauction.com

CONFERENCES, CONVENTIONS, AND CONTINUING EDUCATION

The Folk Art Institute
The American Folk Art Museum
45 West 53rd Street
New York, NY 10019
E-mail:
lkogan@folkartmuseum.org
Web site: www.folkartmuseum.org/

Williamsburg Antiques Forum
Colonial Williamsburg
P. O. Box 1776
Williamsburg, VA 23187
Phone: 757-220-7174
Fax: 757-565-8630
E-mail: tdailey@cwf.org.
Web site: www.history.org/history/
institute/instituto3.cfm

The Dublin Seminar for New England Folklife
Boston University Scholarly
Publications
985 Commonwealth Avenue
Boston, MA 02215
Phone: 617-353-4106
E-mail: dublsem@bu.edu
Web site: www.bu.edu/
dublinseminar/Description.html

CONSERVATORS

Most major museums have a conservation department whose staff either may be allowed to take on outside work on their own time, or who may be able to recommend a local conservator to suit your needs.

Other more general resources and referring agencies include:

The American Institute for Conservation of Historic and Artistic Works
1717 K Street NW, Suite 200
Washington, DC 20006
Phone: 202-452-9545
Fax: 202-452-9328
Web site: www.aic.stanford.edu

Textile Conservation Workshop
3 Main Street
South Salem, NY 10590
Phone: 914-763-5805
Fax: 914-763-5549
E-mail: textile@bestweb.net
Web site: www.rap-arcc.org/
welcome/tcw.htm

University of Delaware Library/ Internet Resources for Art Conservation
Web site: www2.lib.udel.edu/subj/
artc/internet.htm

MAGAZINES AND PERIODICALS

Antiques and the Arts Weekly (A.K.A. The Newtown Bee)
5 Church Hill Road
Newtown, CT 06470
Phone: 203-426-8036
Fax: 203-426-1394
E-mail: info@thebee.com
Web site: www.antiquesandthearts.
com

Art & Auction
11 E. 36th Street, 9th Floor
New York, NY 10016
Phone: 212-447-9555
Advertising Fax: 212-532-5044
Editorial Fax: 212-532-7321
Editorial E-mail: edit@

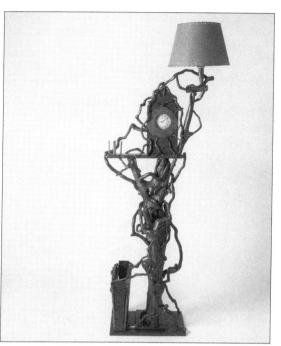

Twig Floor Lamp
c. 1920, North Carolina, by Blowing Rock Artist.
72" H
Photo courtesy Cherry Gallery

Sampler Quilt
Dated 1884, Massachusetts, signed in center "SEC".
Pieced and appliquéd cotton.
80" H × 82" W
Photo courtesy Shelly Zegart; Private collection

artandauction.com
Website: www.artandauction.com

The Catalog of Antiques and Fine Art
125 Walnut Street
Watertown, MA 02472
Phone: local 617-926-0004; national 888-922-0004
Fax: 617-926-0104
E-mail:
csr@AntiquesandFineArt.com
Web site: www.antiquesandfineart.com

Folk Art
American Folk Art Museum
49 West 53rd Street
New York, NY 10019
Phone: 212-977-7170
Fax: 212-977-8134
E-mail: info@folkartmuseum.org
Web site: www.folkartmuseum.org

Intuit
The Center for Intuitive and Outsider Art
756 N. Milwaukee Avenue
Chicago, IL 60622
Phone: 312-243-9088
Fax: 312-243-9089
E mail: intuit@art.org
Web Site: www.outsider.art.org

Maine Antique Digest
P. O. Box 1429
Waldoboro, ME 04572
Phone: local 207-832-7534, national 800-752-8521
Fax: 207-832-7341
E-mail: mad@maine.com
Web Site: www.maineantiquedigest.com

The Magazine Antiques
Brant Publishing
575 Broadway
New York, NY 10012
Phone: 212-941-2800
Fax: 212-941-2897
Web Site:
www.themagazineantiques.com

Raw Vision Magazine
163 Amsterdam Avenue #203
New York, NY 10023
Phone: 212-714-8381
E-mail: info@rawvision.com
Web site: www.rawvision.com/mainmenu.php

Newsletters

The Quilt Connection
Quarterly newsletter with membership to the American Folk Art Museum.

The Folk Art Messenger
Quarterly newsletter with membership to the Folk Art Society in America.

The Outsider
Twice annual publication by Intuit: The Center for Intuitive and Outsider Art.

MUSEUMS

Abby Aldrich Rockefeller Folk Art Center
325 Francis Street
Williamsburg, VA 23185
Phone: 800-447-8679
Web site: www.history.org/history/museums/abby_art.cfm

American Folk Art Museum
45 West 53rd Street
New York, NY 10019
Phone: 212-265-1040
Web site: www.folkartmuseum.org

The American Visionary Art Museum
800 Key Highway
Baltimore, MD 21230
Phone: 410-244-1900
Fax: 410-244-5858
Web site: www.avam.org

Twisted Nose
1987, Georgia, by Bessie Harvey (1929–1994). Polychrome wood. 20"H × 13"W × 9"D Photo courtesy Cavin-Morris Gallery

The Art Institute of Chicago
111 South Michigan Avenue
Chicago, IL 60603
Phone: 312-443-3600
E-mail: webmaster@artic.edu
Web site: www.artic.edu

The Chrysler Museum
245 West Olney Road
Norfolk, VA 23510
Phone: 757-664-6200
Fax: 757-664-6201
E-mail: museum@chrysler.org
Web site: www.chrysler.org/index.
asp

**Heritage Center Museum of
Lancaster County**
13 West King Street
Lancaster, PA 17603
Phone: 717-299-6440
Fax: 717-299-6916
E-mail: heritage@paonline.com
Web site: www.lancasterheritage.
com

Heritage Plantation
67 Grove Street
Sandwich, MA 02563
Phone: 508-888-3300
Fax: 508-888-9535
E-mail:
info@heritagemuseums.org
Web Site: www.
heritagemuseumsandgardens.org

Historic Deerfield, Inc.
Box 321
Deerfield, MA 01342
Phone: 413-774-5581
Fax: 413-775-7220
Web site: www.historic-deerfield.org

International Quilt Study Center
P. O. Box 830838
234 Home Economics Building
University of Nebraska-Lincoln
Lincoln, NE 68583
Phone: 402-472-6549
Fax: 402-472-0640
Web site: www.quiltstudy.uni.edu

John Michael Kohler Arts Center
608 New York Avenue
P. O. Box 489
Sheboygan, WI 53082
Phone: 920-458-6144
Fax: 920-458-4473
Web site: www.jmkac.org

Kentucky Folk Art Center
102 West First Street
Morehead, KY 40351
Phone: 606-783-2204
Fax: 606-783-5034
E-mail: folkart@moreheadstate.edu
Web site: www.kyfolkart.org

**The Menello Museum of
American Folk Art**
900 East Princeton Street
Orlando, FL 32803
Phone: 407-246-4278
Fax: 407-246-4329
Web site: www.menellomuseum.
com

Metropolitan Museum of Art
1000 Fifth Avenue
New York, NY 10028
Phone: 212-535-7710;
TTY: 212-650-2921
Web site: www.metmuseum.org/
home.asp

Milwaukee Art Museum
700 N. Art Museum Drive
Milwaukee, WI 53202
Phone: 414-224-3220
Web site: www.mam.org

Mingei International Museum
P. O. Box 553
La Jolla, CA 92038
Phone: 619-239-0003
Fax: 619-239-0605
E-mail: mingei@mingei.org
Web site: www.mingei.org

The Mint Museum of Art
2730 Randolph Road
Charlotte, NC 28207
Phone: 704-337-2000
Web site: www.mintmuseum.org

Museum of International Folk Art
Museum Hill, Camino Lejo
P. O. Box 2087
Santa Fe, NM 87504
Phone: 505-476-1200
Fax: 505-476-1300
E-mail: info@moifa.org
Web site: www.moifa.org

**National Museum of
American Art**
VB 3100, MRC 970
P. O. Box 37012
Washington, D.C. 20013-7012
Web site: www.americanart.si.edu

New England Quilt Museum
18 Shattuck Street
Lowell, MA 01852
Phone: 978-452-4207
Web site: www.nequiltmuseum.org

The Newark Museum
49 Washington Street
Newark, NJ 07102
Phone: 973-596-655;
TTY: 973-596-6355
E-mail: webmaster@
newarkmuseum.org
Web site: www.newarkmuseum.org

**New York State Historical
Association**
Lake Road
Route 80
Cooperstown, NY 13326
Phone: 607-547-1400;
national 888-547-1450
E-mail: info@nysha.org
Web mail: www.nysha.org

Peabody-Essex Museum
East India Square
Salem, MA 01970
Phone: local 978-745-9500;
national 866-745-1876;
TTY: 978-740-3649
Web site: www.pem.org/homepage

Philadelphia Museum of Art
P. O. Box 7646
Benjamin Franklin Parkway and
26th Street

Philadelphia, PA 19130
Phone: 215-763-8100;
TTY: 215-684-7600
Web site: www.philamuseum.org

Shelburne Museum
U.S. Route 7
P. O. Box 10
Shelburne, VT 05482
Phone: 802-985-3346
Fax: 802-985-2331
E-mail:
info@shelburnemuseum.org
Web site:
www.shelburnemuseum.org

Strawberry Banke Museum
Marcy Street
P. O. Box 300
Portsmouth, NH 03802
Phone: 603-433-1100
Fax: 603-433-1115
E-mail:
hharris@strawberybanke.org
Web site: www.strawberybanke.org

Winterthur
Winterthur Museum, Garden
& Library
Winterthur, DE 19735
Phone: 800-448-3883;
TTY: 302-888-4907
E-mail: webmaster@winterthur.org
Web site: www.winterthur.org

ONLINE RESOURCES

In addition to most museums
and historical societies providing information regarding
artists and objects in their collections, exhibitions, member
events, and public services,
several antiques market–
related Web sites offer both
non-subscriber and subscriber-
based information. The latter
is generally more informative,
and many sites offer sub-
scriber-level information for a

Shooting Gallery Duck
Early twentieth century. Polychrome cast iron. Approximately 5" H
Private collection

Carved Wooden Fan Dancer
c. 1930s, New England. Carved and painted wood. 10" H
Photo courtesy Helga Photo Studio; Private collection

low one-time user fee. As with any database of information, online services are only as good and up-to-date as the information entered; when trying to learn value, it is a good idea to consult more than one service. It is also a good idea to develop relationships with reliable dealers and auction houses. Some helpful sites include:

www.antiquesandtheartsweekly. com

www.artfact.com

www.fineartstrader.com

www.maineantiquedigest.com

www.p4a.com

SHOPS

The Ames Gallery
Bonnie Grossman
2661 Cedar Street
Berkeley, CA 94708
Phone: 510-845-4949
Fax: 510-845-6219
E-mail: info@amesgallery.com
Web site:
www.theamgesgallery.com

American Primitive Gallery
Arne Anton
594 Broadway #205
New York, NY 10012
Phone: 212-966-1530

Augustus Decorative Arts, Ltd.
Elle Shushan
1600 Arch Street #1603
Philadelphia, PA 19103
Phone: 267-514-2033
Fax: 267-514-2034
E-mail: Elle@Portrait-Miniatures.com
Web site: www.Portrait-Miniatures.com

Barbara Ardizone
62 Main Street
P. O. Box 433
Salisbury, CT 06068
Phone/ Fax: 860-435-3057

Ballyhack Antiques
P.O. Box 85
Cornwall, CT 06753
Phone: 860-672-6751
Fax: 860-672-0005
E-mail:
ballyhackantiques@yahoo.com
Web site:
www.ballyhackantiques.com

Pam Boynton, Martha Boynton
82 Pleasant Street
Groton, MA 01450
Phone: 978-448-5031 and 978-597-6794
E-mail: 2ekeb@Prodigy.net

Philip Bradley Antiques
1101 E Lancaster Ave
Downingtown, PA 19335
Phone: 610-269-0427

Hollis E. Brodrick
P. O. Box 30
Portsmouth, NH 03802
Phone: 603-433-7075

Joan Brownstein
24 Parker Street
Newbury, MA 01951

Cavin Morris Gallery
Shari Cavin and Randall Morris
560 Broadway, Suite 405B
New York, NY 10012
Phone: 212-226-3768
Fax: 212-226-0155
E-mail: blugriot@aol.com
Web site: www.cavinmorris.com

Cherry Gallery
Jeff Cherry and Kass Hogan
4 Stissing Mountain Lane
Pine Plains, NY 12567
Phone/Fax: 518-398-7531
E-mail: info@CherryGallery.com
Web site: www.CherryGallery.com

Courcier-Wilkins
Suzanne Courcier and Bob Wilkins
11463 Route 22
Austerlitz, NY 12017
Phone: 518-392-5754

Colette Donovan
98 River Road
Merrimacport, MA 01860
Phone: 978-346-0614
E-mail: ColetteDonovan@
earthlink.net

Epstein/Powell Gallery
Gene Epstein and Kay Powell
22 Wooster Street
New York, NY 10013
Phone: 212-226-7316
Web site: www.soho-ny.com/
epsteinpowell

M. Finkel and Daughter
Morris Finkel and Amy Finkel
936 Pine Street
Philadelphia, PA 19107
Phone: 215-627-7797
Fax: 215-627-8199
E-mail: mailbox@finkelantiques.
com
Web site: www.mfinkelanddaughter.
com

Laura Fisher
1050 Second Avenue, Gallery 84
New York, NY 10022
Phone: 212-838-2596
E-mail: LFAntiqueQuilts@aol.com

Fleisher/Ollman Gallery
John Ollman
1616 Walnut Street, Suite 100
Philadelphia, PA 19103
Phone: 215-545-7562
Fax: 215-545-6140
E-mail: info@fleisher-ollmangallery.
com
Web site: www.fleisher-
ollmangallery.com

Gemini Antiques
Stephen and Leon Weiss
P. O. Box 1752
Bridgehampton, NY 11932
Phone: 631-726-5057
Fax: 631-726-9366
E-mail:
julgert@geminiantiques.com
Web: www.geminiantiques.com

Fred Giampetro
153 1/2 Bradley Street
New Haven, CT 06511
Phone: 203-787-3851
Fax: 203-787-1431

James and Nancy Glazer
P. O. Box 222
Bailey Island, ME 04003
Phone: 207-833-6973
E-mail: glazer@clinic.net

RJG Antiques
Russ and Karen Goldberger
P. O. Box 60
Rye, NH 03870
Phone: 603-433-1770
Fax: 603-433-3937
E-mail: antiques@rjgantiques.com
Web: www.rjgantiques.com

**David L. Good/Samuel W.
Forsythe Antiques**
7887 State Route 177
Camden, OH 45311
Phone: 513-796-2693

Carl Hammer Gallery
200 West Superior
Chicago, IL 60610
Phone: 312-266-8512
Fax: 312-266-8510

Harvey Art & Antiques
Harvey Pranian
1328 Greenleaf Street
Evanston, IL 60202
Phone: 847-866-6766
Fax: 847-866-6880
E-mail: harvey@harveyantiques.
com

Heller Washam Antiques
Don Heller
1235 Congress Street
Portland, ME 04102
Phone: 207-773-8288

Nina Hellman Marine Antiques
48 Centre Street
Nantucket, MA 02554
Phone: 508-228-4677
Fax: 508-228-1934
E-mail: marantqs@nantucket.net

Samuel Herrup Antiques
P. O. Box 248
435 Sheffield Plain Road
Sheffield, MA 02157
Phone: 413-229-0424
Fax: 413-229-2829
E-mail: ssher@ben.net

Hill Gallery
Timothy and Pamela Hill
407 West Brown Street
Birmingham, MI 48009
Phone: 248-540-9288
Fax: 248-540-6965
E-mail: hillgallery@earthlink.net

Wayne and Phyllis Hilt
RR 1
Haddam Neck, CT 06424
Phone: 860-267-2146
Fax: 860-267-9541
E-mail: philt@snet.net

Stephen & Carol Huber
40 Ferry Road
Old Saybrook, CT 06475
Phone: 860-388-6809
Fax: 860-434-9709
E-mail:
hubers@antiquesamplers.com
Web: www.antiquesamplers.com

Hyland-Granby
Alan Granby
P. O. Box 457
Hyannisport, MA 02647
Phone: 508-771-3070

Fax: 508-778-4842
E-mail: hgmarine@capecod.net
Web: www.hylandgranby.com

Allan and Penny Katz Americana
25 Old Still Road
Woodbridge, CT 06525
Phone: 203-393-9356
E-mail: folkkatz@optonline.net

Kelter-Malcé
Jolie Kelter and Michael Malcé
74 Jane Street
New York, NY 10014
Phone: 212-675-7380
Fax: 212-675-9529
E-mail: keltermalce@mac.com

Greg K. Kramer & Co.
27 West Freeman Street
Robesonia, PA 19551
Phone: 610-693-3223
Fax: 610-693-3433

Nathan Liverant and Son Antiques
Arthur Liverant
P. O. Box 103
Colchester, CT 06415
Phone: 860-537-2409
Fax: 860-537-0577
E-mail:
nliverantandson@biz.ctol.net

Gloria Lonergan
P. O. Box 299
Mendham, NJ 07945
Phone: 973-543-2133
Fax: 973-543-8286
E-mail: pg.lonergan@verizon.net

Judith and James Milne, Inc.
506 East 74th Street
New York, NY 10021
Phone: 212-472-0107
Fax: 212-472-1481
E-mail: milneinc@aol.com
Web site: www.milneantiques.com

David C. Morey
161 Main Street
P. O. Box 368
Thomaston, ME 04861
Phone: 207-354-6033
Fax: 207-354-3611
E-mail: acm@midcoast.com

Thurston Nichols American Antiques LLC
522 Twin Ponds Road
Breinigsville, PA 18031
Phone: 610-395-5154
Fax: 610-395-3679
E-mail: thurston@fast.net
Web site: www.antiques101.com

Stephen O'Brien, Jr. (decoys)
268 Newbury Street
Boston, MA 02116
Phone: 617-536-0536
E-mail: info@americansportin-gart.com
Web site: www.americansportingart.com

Olde Hope Antiques, Inc.
Patrick Bell and Edwin Hild
P. O. Box 718
New Hope, PA 18938
Phone: 215-297-0200
Fax: 215-297-0300
E-mail: info@oldehope.com
Web site: www.oldehope.com

Susan Parrish
390 Bleecker Street
New York, NY 10014
Phone: 212-645-5020
E-mail: susanparrishny@aol.com

Frank and Barbara Pollack
American Antiques & Art
1214 Green Bay Road
Highland Park, IL 60035
Phone: 847-433-2213
E-mail: fpollack@compuserve.com
Web site: www.maineantiquedigest.com/adimg/pollack.htm

Sumpter Priddy III, Inc.
601 S. Washington Street
Alexandria, VA 22314
Phone: 703-299-0800
Fax: 703-299-9688
E-mail: stp@sumpterpriddy.com
Web site: www.sumpterpriddy.com

Raccoon Creek, LLC
George R. Allen and Gordon L. Wyckoff
P. O. Box 457
20 Main Street
Bridgeport, NJ 08014
Phone: 856-467-3197
Fax: 856-467-3431
E-mail: raccooncreek@msn.com
Web site: www.maineantiquedigest.com/adimg/raccoon.htm

Jackie Radwin American Antiques and Folk Art
1 Dorchester Place
San Antonio, TX 78209
Phone: 210-824-7711 or 210-240-1621
Fax: 210-930-5452
E-mail: jr@onr.com
Web site: www.jackieradwin.com

Ricco/Maresca Gallery
Roger Ricco and Frank Maresca
529 West 20th Street, 3rd Floor
New York, NY 10011
Phone: 212-627-4819
Fax: 212-627-5117
E-mail: info@riccomaresca.com
Web site: www.riccomaresca.com

Luise Ross Gallery
568 Broadway, Suite #402
New York, NY 10012
Phone: 212 343-2161
Fax: 212 343-2468
E-mail: lrossgallery@earthlink.net
Web site: www.luiserossgallery.com

Stella Rubin
12300 Glen Road
Potomac, MD 20854
Phone: 301-948-4187

Group of Early 20th Century Spruce Gum Boxes
Found in Maine. Hand carved and decorated. Ranging in size from 6" H × 4" W × 2" D to 3" H × 2" W × ¹/₂" W Private collection

Fax: 301-948-0460
E-mail: stella.rubin@att.net
Web site: www.stellarubin.com

John Keith Russell Antiques
P. O. Box 414
110 Spring Street
South Salem, NY 10590
Phone: 914-763-8144
Fax: 914-763-3553
E-mail: jkrantique@aol.com

Peter Sawyer
16 Court Street
Exeter, NH 03833
Phone: 603-772-5279
E-mail: pjscream@aol.com

David Schorsch American Antiques, Inc.
244 Main Street South
Woodbury, CT 06798
Phone: 203-263-3131
Fax: 203-263-2622

Stephen Score, Inc.
73 Chestnut Street
Boston, MA 02108
Phone: 617-227-9192

Cheryl & Paul Scott
232 Bear Hill Road
P. O. Box 835
Hillsborough, NH 03244
Phone: 603-464-3617
Fax: 603-464-5837

Lewis W. Scranton
38 Firetower Road
Killingsworth, CT 06419
Phone: 860-663-1060

John Sideli Art & Antiques
880 Mitchell Street
Hillsdale, NY 12529
Phone: 518-325-6747
Fax: 518-325-7447

Elliott and Grace Snyder Antiques
P. O. Box 598
37 Undermountain Road
South Egremont, MA 01258
Phone: 413-528-3581
Fax: 413-528-3586
E-mail: zorvis@bcn.net

George and Debbie Spiecker
P. O. Box 40
North Hampton, NH 03862
Phone: 603-964-4738
E-mail: fineamericana@aol.com
Web site: www.fineamericana.com

Stephen-Douglas Antiques
Stephen Corrigan and
Douglas Jackman
7 Meetinghouse Road
P. O. Box 27
Rockingham, VT 05101
Phone: 802-463-4296

Jeffrey Tillou Antiques
Box 1609
33 West Street
Litchfield, CT 06759
Phone: 860-567-9693
Fax: 860-567-2781
Web site: www.tillouantiques.com

Van Tassel-Bauman /American Antiques
Ruth J. Van Tassel-Baumann
Donald O. Baumann
690 Sugartown Road
Malvern, PA 19355
Phone: 610-647-3339
E-mail: rvtstitches@aol.com
Web site: www.AntiquesAndFineArt.com/tasselbaumann

Clifford Wallach
81 Washington Street, Suite 7J
Brooklyn, NY 11201
Phone: 718-596-5325
E-mail: info@trampart.com
Web site: www.trampart.com

Walters-Benisek
Don Walters and Mary Benisek
1 Amber Lane
Northampton, MA 01060
Phone: 413-586-3909

Victor Weinblatt
P. O. Box 835
South Hadley, MA 01075
Phone: 413-533-6435
Fax: 413-535-2303
At Shows Only

David Wheatcroft
26 West Main Street
Westborough, MA 01581
Phone: 508-366-1723
Fax: 508-366-9301
E-mail:
mailbox@davidwheatcroft.com
Web site: www.davidwheatcroft.com

Jan Whitlock Textiles
P. O. Box 583
Chadds Ford, PA 19317
Phone: 302-655-1117
E-mail: JanWhitlock@aol.com
Web site:
www.JanWhitlockTextiles.com

Woodard and Greenstein
Thomas K. Woodard and Blanche
Greenstein
506 East 74th Street, 5th floor
New York, NY 10021
Phone: 212-988-2906
Fax: 212-734-9663
Web site: www.woodardweave.com

Melinda and Laszlo Zongor
4862 Bedford Valley Road
Bedford, PA 15522
Phone: 814-356-3777
E-mail: Coverlets@pennswoods.net

SHOW PROMOTERS

For a list of show promotion information in your area, consult
the Professional Show Manager's Association, Inc (PSMA).

**Professional Show Manager's
Association, Inc.**
C. Mitchell Sorensen, Executive
Director

1 Regency Drive, P. O. Box 30
Bloomfield, CT 06002
Phone: 860-243-3977
Fax: 860-286-0787
E-mail: Msorensen@SSMGT.COM
Web site: www.psmashows.org

Also consult your local newspa-
pers, and the periodicals referred to
in Magazines and Periodicals as
well as the list below.

Mid-Atlantic

Melvin L. Arion
P. O. Box 119
Laurel, DE 19956
Phone: 302-875-5326

Armacost Antiques Shows, Ltd.
600 Edgevale Road
Baltimore, MD 21210
Phone and fax: 410-435-2292
E-mail:
Bob@ArmacostAntiquesShows.
com
Web site:
www.armacostantiquesshows.com

Jim Burk Antique Shows
3012 Miller Road
Washington Boro, PA 17582
Phone: 717-872-2778
E-mail: jrburk1@comcast.net
Web site:
www.jimburkantiqueshows.com

Barry M. Cohen/ B4R Time, Inc
P. O. Box 9095
Alexandria, VA 22304
Phone: 703- 914-1268
Fax: 703- 914-1268
E-mail: b4rtime@cox.net
Web site: www.psmashows.org

**Goodrich & Company
Promotions, Inc.**
P. O. Box 1577
Mechanicsburg, PA 17055
Phone: 717-796-2380
Fax: 717-796-2384

Carved Wood Tramp Art Picture Frame with Silhouettes, Daguerreotypes and Marriage Certificate
Early twentieth century, Pennsylvania. Inscribed "Johannes George Miller to Susanna Benner(in) was married the 30th day of May 1825 by Herr Pastor Bauer." Polychrome rectangular frame with reverse painted on glass silhouette portraits above six daguerreotype portraits, with chip carving around frames and molding. 42" H × 19" W Private collection

Paint-Decorated Pine Checker/Parcheesi Game Board
Late nineteenth century, New England. Two-sided game board with original polychrome finish and brass ring handle. 25³/4" H × 25⁵/8" W Private collection

E-mail: info@goodrichpromo-
tions.com
Web site: www.goodrichpromotions.
com

**Keeling Wainwright Associates,
Inc.**
P. O. Box 333
Cabin John, MD 20818
Phone: 301-263-9314
E-mail: info@blackfineartshow.com

Shador Pappabello
P. O. Box 12069
Silver Spring, MD 20908
Phone: 301-933-6994
Fax: 301-933-1072
E-mail: shadorant@aol.com
Web site: www.pappabello.com

Midwest

Krause Publications
700 East State Street
Iola, WI 54990
Phone: 715-445-2214
Fax: 715-445-4087
Web site:
www.krause.com/static/shows.htm

Northeast

**Antique Dealers Association
Show**
ADA Inc
P. O. Box 335
Greens Farms, CT 06838
E-mail: info@adadealers.com
Web site: www.adadealers.com

Brimfield's Heart-O-The-Mart
Tracey Healy
P. O. Box 26
Brimfield, MA 01010
Phone: 413-245-9556
Fax: 413-245-3542
E-mail: info@brimfield-hotm.com
Web site: www.brimfield-hotm.com

**Frank Gaglio/Barn Star
Productions**
7 Center Street

Rhinebeck, NY 12572
Phone: 845-876-0616
Fax: 845-876-8271
E-mail: barnstar1@aol.com
Web site: www.barnstar.com

**Marilyn Gould/MICG Antiques
Promotions**
10 Chicken Street
Wilton, CT 06897
Phone: 203-762-3525

Madison-Bouckville Mgt.
P. O. Box 97
Hamilton, NY 13346
Phone: 315-824-2462
Fax: 315-824-4511
Web site:
www.bouckvilleantiqueshows.com

**The New Hampshire Antiques
Dealers Association**
E-mail: nhada@rcn.com
Web site: www.nhada.org

Jacqueline Sideli Productions
500 State Avenue,
Fall River, MA 02724
Phone; 508-324-4900
E-mail: sidelishow@aol.com

Sanford L. Smith & Associates
68 East 7th Street
New York, NY 10003
Phone: 212-777-5218
Fax: 212-477-6490
E-mail: info@sanfordsmith.com
Web site: www.sanfordsmith.com

**Stella Show Management
Company**
151 West 25th Street, Suite 2
New York, NY 10001
Phone: 212-255-0020
Fax: 212-255-0002
E-mail: stellashows@aol.com
Web site: www.stellashows.com

**Vermont Antiques Dealers'
Association**
Web site: www.vermontada.com

Wendy Antiques Shows
P. O. Box 707
Rye, NY 10580
Phone: 914-698-3442
Fax: 914-698-6273
E-mail: e.maloney@bmcorp.com
Web site:
www.wendyantiquesshows.com

Winter Antiques Show
Catherine Sweeney Singer,
Show Director
337 Alexander Avenue
Bronx, NY 10454
Phone: 718-292-7392 or
718-665-5250
Fax: 718-665-5532
E-mail:
info@winterantiquesshow.com
Web site:
www.winterantiquesshow.com

Southeast

DMG World Media/Art and Antiques Shows, North America
1555 Palm Beach Lakes Blvd,
Suite 200
West Palm Beach, FL 33401
Phone: 561-640-3433
Fax: 561-640-3266
E-mail: webmaster@
dmgworldmedia.com
Web site: www.dmgworldmedia.
com/index2.html

Heart of Country
Richard E. Kramer & Assoc.
427 Midvale Ave
St. Louis, MO 63130
Phone: 800-862-1090
Fax: 314-862-1094
Web site: www.heartofcountry.com

Heritage Promotions
P. O. Box 3504
Lynchburg, VA 24503
Phone: 434-846-7452 or
434-847-8242

Bob Smith & Dolphin Promotions Inc.
P. O. Box 7320
Fort Lauderdale, FL 33338
Phone: 954-563-6747
Fax: 954-566-1982
E-mail: DolphinPromotions@
worldnet.att.net
Web site: www.dolphinfairs.com

Southwest

John R. Sauls
P. O. Box 448
Tyler, TX 75710
Phone: 800-947-5799
Fax: 800-999-2148
E-mail: johnsauls@tyler.net
Web site:
www.roundtop-marburger.com

Emma Lee Turney, Antiques Productions
P. O. Box 821289
Houston, TX 77282
Phone: 281-493-5501
Fax: 281-293-0320
E-mail: turnyshows@aol.com
Web site:
www.roundtopantiquesfair.com

Whitehawk Associates, Inc.
Box 1272
Santa Fe, NM 87504-1272
Phone: 505-992-8929 Fax: 505-986-0051
E-mail: whitehawk02@hotmail.com
Web site: www.pueblopottery.com/
whawk.htm

West

The Antique Dealers Association of California
110 Pacific
Box 271
San Francisco, CA 94111-1900
Phone: 415-398-8115
Web site:
www.antiquedealersca.com

California Country Antique Show
Tom Baker
P. O. Box 495
Soquel, CA 95073
Phone: 831-479-4404
E-mail: tom@bakercoantiques.com
Web site:
www.californiacountryshow.com

Caskey-Lees
P. O. Box 1409
Topanga, CA 90290
Phone: 310-455-2886
E-mail: info@caskeylees.com
Web site: www.caskeylees.com

Palmer/Wirfs & Associates
4001 NE Halsey
Portland, OR 97232
Phone: 503-282-0877
Fax: 503-282-2953
E-mail: palmerwirfs@qwest.net
Web site: www.palmerwirfs.com

Spirit of Country Antiques Show
Kathy Hind/Linda Carr
Phone: 425-883-1896
E-mail:
kathy@spiritofcountryantiques.com
Web site:
www.spiritofcountryantiques.com

SUPPLIES

Any hardware store, photo supply shop, or fabric store will stock most of the basic supplies you will need (see Chapter 6, Think and Talk Like an Expert, Section 5 "Essential Tools of Collecting"). The following conservation suppliers carry more hard-to-find or specialized tools and materials.

Archivart
7 Caesar Place
Moonachie, NJ 07074
Phone: 800-804-8428
E-mail: sales@archivart.com
Web site: www.archivart.com

Conservation Resources International, LLC
5532 Port Royal Road
Springfield, VA 22151
Phone: local 703-321-7730; national 800-634-6932
Fax: 703-321-0629
E-mail:
criusa@conservationresources.com
Web site:
www.conservationresources.com

Conservation Support Systems
P. O. Box 91746
Santa Barbara, CA 93190
Phone: local 805-682-9843; national 800-482-6299
Fax: 805-682-2064
E-mail: css@silcom.com
Web site: www.silcom.com/~css

Gaylord Brothers
Box 4901
Syracuse, NY 13221
Phone: local 315-634-8471, national 800-448-6160
Fax: local 315-457-0564, national 800-272-3412
E-mail:
customerservice@gaylord.com
Web site: www.gaylord.com

Hollinger Corporation
9401 Northeast Drive
Fredericksburg, VA 22408
Phone: 800-634-0491
Fax: 800-947-8814
E-mail: GenealogyStore@aol.com
Web site: www.
genealogicalstorageproducts.com/
index.html

Light Impressions Corp.
P. O. Box 787
Brea, CA 92822
Tel: 800-828-6216
Fax: 800-828-5539

Hollow-cut Silhouette and Watercolor Miniature Portraits
Early nineteenth century, New England. Hollow-cut and watercolors on paper, in original frames. 6" H × 4" W Private collection

Group of Early 20th Century New England Children's Toys
Wooden crow pull toy, painted black. 24" H Polychrome wooden duck squeak toy with wooden wheels. 8" H Mechanical polychrome papier-mâché and fabric rabbit. 24" H Photo courtesy Helga Photo Studio; Private collection

E-mail:
LiWebsite@limpressions.com
Web site:
www.lightimpressionsdirect.com

MasterPak
145 East 57th Street
New York, NY 10022
Phone: 800-922-5522
Fax: 212-586-6961
E-mail: mpak@masterpak-usa.com
Web site: www.masterpak-usa.com

Talas
568 Broadway
New York, NY 10002

Phone: 212-219-0770
Fax: 212-219-0735
E-mail: info@talas-nyc.com
Web site: www.talas-nyc.com

University Products, Inc.
517 Main Street
P. O. Box 101
Holyoke, MA 04041
Phone: 800.336.4847
Fax: 800.532.9281
E-mail:
custserv@universityproducts.com
Web site:
www.universityproducts.com

THE INSTANT EXPERT QUIZ

The following questions and answers should help you to review points made in this book.

1. What was the first American folk art?

2. Identify three forms in American folk art that are products of teaching institutions.

3. How are redware and stoneware similar? How are they different?

4. Why are Amish quilts designed in geometric color blocks?

5. Identify a central theme to Shaker furniture and decorative arts.

6. Identify a fundamental cultural difference between the Shakers and Amish and how that affects their decorative arts.

7. Who are the following collectors and what museum is now home to their collection?

   • Ima Hogg

   • Jean and Howard Lipman

   • Abby Aldrich Rockefeller

   • Martha and Max Karolik

   • Eleanor and Mabel van Alstyne

   • Electra Havemeyer Webb

   • Henry Francis du Pont

   • Edgar William and Bernice Chrysler Garbisch

   • Gertrude Vanderbilt Whitney

8. What contributions did the following make to American folk art?

   • Faith and Edward Deming Andrews

   • Elie Nadelman

- Edith Gregor Halpert
- Alice Winchester
- Juliana Force
- Mary Black
- Nina Fletcher Little
- Holger Cahill

9. Identify the following names:
   - Wilhelm Schimmel
   - Edward Hicks
   - Ammi Phillips
   - Erastus Salisbury Field
   - Conrad Mumbauer
   - Moses Eaton
   - Crolius Family
   - William Matthew Prior
   - Horace Pippin
   - Francis Portzline
   - Grandma Moses
   - Susan Waters
   - Shem Drowne
   - J. W. Fiske
   - Thomas Matteson
   - E. & L. Norton
   - Jacob Medinger
   - Winthrop Chandler
   - Samuel A. and Ruth W. Shute
   - Joseph Whiting Stock
   - James Sanford Ellsworth
   - Johannes Spitler
   - Henry Lapp

- John and James Bard
- A. L. Jewell
- L. W. Cushing
- Samuel Folwell
- William Edmondson
- Bill Traylor
- Samuel Robb

10. Answer the following questions true or false:

_____ Regionalism influences American folk art

_____ Some examples of American folk art have European antecedents

_____ Eunice Pinney is a twentieth-century Outsider Artist

_____ Thomas Matteson is a Vermont paint-decorated furniture artist

_____ Moses Eaton is a Vermont paint-decorated furniture artist

_____ William Edmondson is known for his vivid abstracts on brown paper

_____ Prints were often the source for watercolors and oil paintings

_____ Painted tinware is toleware

_____ Edward Hicks is best known as a portrait painter

_____ Native Americans were the first decoy makers

11. In what areas of output are the following people most well known?

- Edward Sands Frost
- Frederick Otto Krebs
- Winthrop Chandler
- Joseph Hidley
- Laban Beecher
- Lothrop T. Holmes

- Ralph and Martha Cahoon
- A. Elmer Crowell
- James Henry Wright
- Joseph Davis
- Morris Hirshfield
- The Dentzel Family
- J. Howard & Co.
- John Blunt
- John Bellamy
- Julius Theodore Melchers
- Aaron Mountz
- Durs Rudy
- Samuel Bentz
- Ruth Henshaw Bascom
- Hannah Davis
- Rufus Hathaway
- John Bell
- John Brewster
- Miles Carpenter
- John Remmey
- Rufus Porter
- Ann Butler
- Sheldon Peck
- Jacob Maentel
- Jurgan F. Huge
- J.O.J. Frost
- Charles Hoffman
- Lem & Steve Ward
- Asahel Powers
- Deborah Goldsmith

- Sturtevant Hamblen
- Fritz Vogt
- Emily Eastman
- Mary Ann Willson
- Gus Wilson
- Hannah Otis
- Joe Lincoln
- Martin Ramirez
- Judith Scott
- Reuben Moulthrop
- John Reber
- Anthony Baecher
- Lanier Meaders
- John Flory
- Henry Leach
- Henry Young
- Zedekiah Belknap
- David Spinner
- Joshua Johnson
- William Jennys
- George Huebner
- Noah North
- Jonathan Fisher
- John Bradley
- M. W. Hopkins
- Elizabeth Perkins
- A. Ellis
- Christian Seltzer
- John Kane
- Elder Henry Green

- Richard Brunton
- John Rassmussen
- John Dilley
- Frederick Myrick
- Elijah Pierce
- Minnie Evans
- Johannes Bard
- The Cross-Legged Angel Artist
- Heinrich Otto
- James Hampton
- William Hawkins
- Adolf Wolfli

12. Identify a source book for each of the following categories:
    - scrimshaw
    - hooked rugs
    - fraktur
    - quilts
    - samplers
    - cigar store figures
    - paint-decorated furniture
    - redware
    - decoys
    - paintings
    - portraits
    - stoneware
    - weathervanes

13. Why were trade signs so important in early American culture?

14. What was the purpose and origin of cigar store figures, and why were Indians most often used as a symbol for the tobacconist?

15. What are the differences among weathervanes, whirligigs, and bannerettes?

16. Describe at least two different types of weathervanes and how they are constructed.

17. In examining a weathervane, what factors would you consider in determining that the object you are looking at is of the period and not a reproduction or fake?

18. Why were more portraits than landscapes painted?

19. Identify the distinguishing features of a folk painting.

20. Why should American tinware not be called toleware? Name at least two ways American tinware was decorated.

21. List at least three motifs used for decoration by the Pennsylvania Germans.

22. List at least three different materials used in the making of baskets.

23. Describe at least two ways Native American baskets are decorated.

24. What are the differences among shirred, yarn sewn, and hooked rugs?

25. Name at least four common stitches in American needlework and their distinguishing features.

26. Why was furniture grain painted? How was it done? How does it differ from marbleizing and smoke decoration?

27. What is slip and how is an object slip decorated?

28. What is sgraffito?

29. Define scrimshaw and identify who made it.

30. What is chalkware, when was it made, and why was it popular?

31. List four resources to which you would turn to better understand a weathervane and its price.

32. Regarding ship carvers: What is a sternboard? What is a figurehead?

Redware Plate
c. 1840, attributed to Rahway Pottery, New Jersey. Coggle edge presentation plate with an unusual and rare manganese slip trailed script decoration with the name "Mary." 11¹/₂" Dia
Photo courtesy Raccoon Creek Antiques

Redware Slip Decorated Loaf Pan
Mid-eighteenth century, northeastern United States. Large serving pan with coggle edge. 18" H × 12" W × 3" D
Photo courtesy Raccoon Creek Antiques

33. Discuss the stylistic characteristics of Ammi Phillips's paintings.

34. What is meant by "schoolgirl" art?

35. Name ten of the most common quilt patterns.

Answers

1. Native American decoys, weathervanes, or gravestone carvings are all acceptable answers.

2. Needlework samplers; calligraphy drawings; theorem paintings.

3. Redware and stoneware are both earthenwares.

   Redware pottery is made from red, native clay, which is porous and brittle, so it is easily cracked and chipped. Since redware was inexpensive to produce, it was widely used every day in the household. Being inexpensive dictated its use most often in the kitchen and dairy. Redware is decorated in a variety of ways: lead is the primary glazing ingredient, with oxides of manganese producing brown-aubergine-black tones and copper producing green tones. Redware could also be slip-decorated and sgraffito-decorated. Redware is fired at a relatively low temperature and is fragile.

   In contrast, stoneware is fired at a very high temperature so as to vitrify. It is dense, durable, will hold liquid even without glazing, and is impervious to acids. Stoneware is made of a combination of clay and a fusible stone, usually feldspar. Most commonly, American stoneware is salt glazed, a technique accomplished by firing the ware first at a low temperature. It was then brought to its highest point and shoveling or throwing hot common salt through the opening at the top of the kiln added the glaze. The high temperature within caused the salt to explode in a vapor, which combined with the free silica in the clay body and covered the pottery with a thin, mottled glaze. When the stoneware was finished, its surface was slightly pitted, like an orange. The action of the salt affected only that portion of the pot exposed to its vapor. Stoneware makers decorated their pots by incising lines or patterns in them or by brushing or trailing designs in cobalt blue or brown slip on them. Incised decoration is most often found on stoneware made before 1825, while slip decoration even appears on very late examples. In a few rare instances, stoneware pottery was decorated with molded and applied figures, especially in the late nineteenth century.

4. With religious beliefs prohibiting the imitation of any of God's creations, it would be considered blasphemy in the Amish community for a quilter to cut and appliqué the kinds of representational motifs, such as a flower, onto their own quilts. As geometric blocks do not represent anything in nature, they are acceptable to produce. Decorative quilting, such as flowers, is acceptable because it is "invisible."

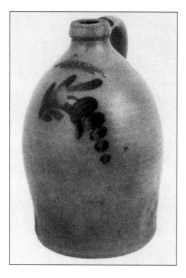

5. In keeping with the Shaker tenet of "Hands to work, hearts to God," Shaker furniture is distinguished by simplicity (decoration was a sign of frivolity or arrogance), utility (anything which didn't accomplish a useful purpose was a distraction), and efficiency (productiveness was evidence of faith and devotion). Any of these three themes are acceptable answers.

6. Inherently, the Shakers were a progressive community whose emphasis on efficiency and its benefits in technology directly impacted the utility, simple appearance, and often multifunctional nature of their decorative arts. In contrast, central to the beliefs of many Amish communities, is an explicit prohibition of the use or ownership of the latest technology. It is a community, therefore, whose decorative arts look backward in their expression of a need to preserve tradition. Were the Shakers extant today, their beliefs would not have prohibited them, for example, from driving a car. Many Amish, as anyone who has driven in Southeastern Pennsylvania knows, still use a traditional horse and buggy.

7. Ima Hogg: Texas collector who gave Bayou Bend to the Museum of Fine Arts, Houston; Jean and Howard Lipman: New York City collectors who gave American folk art to the Whitney Museum of American Art and the American Folk Art Museum, both in New York City; Abby Aldrich

Two-Gallon Stoneware Jug
Mid-nineteenth century, Pennsylvania Impressed "Cowden and Wilcox, Harrisburg, PA," with foliate decoration. 11$\frac{1}{2}$" H
Photo courtesy Pook & Pook

Three-Gallon Stoneware Crock
Mid-nineteenth century, Pennsylvania. With inscription "T. P. Reppert Successor to James Hamilton and Co., Manufacturer, Greensboro, PA." 13" H
Photo courtesy Pook & Pook

Paint-Decorated Shaker One-Door Storage Cupboard
Late eighteenth century, possibly originally constructed to fit in the meetinghouse at Sabbathday Lake, Maine (built in 1794), or the house at Canterbury, New Hampshire (built in 1792).
Pine cupboard retaining an old blue painted surface over a red painted surface with hand wrought hinges and a heavy raised panel surrounded with quarter round molded stiles that are found only on the earliest of Shaker case furniture. $7^{1}/_{2}$" H × 35" W × $16^{1}/_{2}$" D
Photo courtesy John Keith Russell Antiques

Rockefeller: New York City collector who founded the Abby Aldrich Rockefeller Folk Art Center at Colonial Williamsburg, Williamsburg, Virginia; Martha and Max Karolik: Boston, Massachusetts collectors who gave American art collections to the Museum of Fine Arts, Boston; Eleanor and Mabel van Alstyne: collectors who gave American folk art to the Smithsonian Institution, Washington, D.C.; Electra Havemeyer Webb: New York City and Vermont founder-collector of the Shelburne Museum, Shelburne, Vermont; Henry Francis du Pont: Wilmington, Delaware, founder-collector of the Winterthur Museum, Winterthur, Delaware; Edgar William and Bernice Chrysler Garbisch: Maryland collectors who gave part of their collection to the National Museum of American Art in Washington, D.C., and the Whitney Museum of American Art in New York City; Gertrude Vanderbilt Whitney: New York City collector-founder of the Whitney Museum of American Art.

8. Their contributions are as follows:

   • Faith and Edward Deming Andrews: pioneering collectors of Shaker art who documented those decorative arts in their books and exhibitions;

Shaker Trestle Base Dining Table, c. 1840 Acquired at the Shaker community at Canterbury, New Hampshire but resembles tables made at Watervliet, New York. Two board pine top on a birch base retaining an old stained and shellacked finish with the birch trestle through mortised and pinned where the uprights meet the top supports, center trestle, and at the arched base. 28¼"H × 90"L × 33"W Photo courtesy John Keith Russell Antiques

Shaker Sewing Desk, c. 1861, Canterbury, New Hampshire, attributed to Elder Eli Kidder (1783–1867). Pine and maple retaining an old stain and shellacked surface, with an upper gallery of six drawers divided by a single paneled door above a work surface with pull-out extra work surface. The base section has three narrow drawers on the front facade and three shallow full-width drawers on the right facade, all supported on four classical turned Shaker legs. 38½"H × 27"W × 22 × ⅛"D Photo courtesy John Keith Russell Antiques

- Elie Nadelman: celebrated early twentieth-century sculptor inspired by American folk art;

- Edith Gregor Halpert: New York City dealer who formed several important American folk art collections and forged one of the market links between American folk art and contemporary American art;

- Alice Winchester: *Antiques* magazine editor-in-chief and American folk art advocate who co-curated the 1974 Whitney Museum of American Art exhibition, "Flowering of American Folk Art";

- Juliana Force: Gertrude Vanderbilt Whitney's assistant who managed the Whitney Studio Club and then the Whitney Museum of American Art;

- Mary Black: American folk art advocate who curated several of the earliest and most groundbreaking exhibitions on American folk art;

- Nina Fletcher Little: collector whose publications on New England folk art, including the first published catalog of the Abby Aldrich Rockefeller folk art collection, earned her wide respect, and the majority of whose collection is now at the Society for the Preservation of New England Antiquities;

- Holger Cahill: groundbreaking curator who mounted the first major museum exhibitions on American folk art, who forged an historical connection between American folk art and contemporary art, who worked with Edith Gregor Halpert in forming several important private collections of American folk art, and who went on to lead the Works Progress Administration's Federal Art Project.

- Wilhelm Schimmel: mid–late nineteenth-century Pennsylvania wood carver;

- Edward Hicks: second quarter nineteenth-century Bucks County, Pennsylvania, Quaker missionary and allegorical painter;

- Ammi Phillips: second quarter nineteenth-century itinerant portrait painter working in the Massachusetts, Connecticut, and New York border area;

- Erastus Salisbury Field: second quarter nineteenth-century New England itinerant portrait painter;

- Conrad Mumbauer: early nineteenth-century Bucks County, Pennsylvania, redware potter;

- Moses Eaton: New Hampshire artist whose stencil embellishments are seen on walls and paint-decorated furniture;

- Crolius Family: family of New York City stoneware potters active in the eighteenth century;

- William Matthew Prior: second quarter nineteenth-century Boston-based itinerant portrait painter;

- Horace Pippin: early twentieth-century African-American history painter;

- Francis Portzline: second quarter nineteenth-century southeastern Pennsylvania fraktur artist;

- Grandma Moses: twentieth-century memory painter from upstate New York;

- Susan Waters: nineteenth-century still, animal, and portrait painter;

- Shem Drowne: eighteenth-century Boston weathervane maker, maker of the Fanueil Hall Grasshopper weathervane;

- J. W. Fiske: late nineteenth-century New York City iron works foundry;

- Thomas Matteson: Vermont paint-decorated furniture artist circa 1815;

- E. & L. Norton: prolific nineteenth-century Vermont stoneware pottery;

- Jacob Medinger: late nineteenth-century Bucks County, Pennsylvania, redware potter;

- Winthrop Chandler: late eighteenth-century itinerant New England portrait painter;

- Samuel A. and Ruth W. Shute: second quarter nineteenth-century New England and New York husband and wife watercolor portrait artists;

- Joseph Whiting Stock: second quarter nineteenth-century New England itinerant portrait artist;

- James Sanford Ellsworth: second quarter nineteenth-century New England itinerant watercolor portrait artist;

- Johannes Spitler: late eighteenth–early nineteenth-century German-born paint-decorated furniture maker who settled in Virginia;

- Henry Lapp: nineteenth century Pennsylvania furniture maker;

- John and James Bard: New York City–based twin brothers who painted paddle wheel boats on the Hudson River in the mid-nineteenth century;

- A. L. Jewell: Waltham, Massachusetts, based mid-nineteenth century weathervane maker;

- L. W. Cushing: mid–late nineteenth-century Massachusetts weathervane maker;

- Samuel Folwell: Philadelphia-based early nineteenth-century schoolteacher whose recognizable patterns appear in silk pictures of the era;

- William Edmondson: twentieth-century African-American Southern visionary sculptor whose limestone creations populated the landscape around his home;

- Bill Traylor: twentieth-century African-American Southern abstract painter whose scenes of everyday life are usually done in bright colors on cardboard;

- Samuel Robb: New York City late nineteenth-century carver of tobacconist figures.

10. True; True; False; True; False; False; True; False; False; True.

11. They are known for the following, respectively:
    - Edward Sands Frost: hooked rugs;
    - Frederick Otto Krebs: fraktur;
    - Winthrop Chandler: portraiture;
    - Joseph Hidley: landscape painting;
    - Laban Beecher: marine sculpture;
    - Lothrop T. Holmes: decoy making;
    - Ralph and Martha Cahoon: fantasy painting;

- A. Elmer Crowell: decoy making;
- James Henry Wright: marine painter;
- Joseph Davis: watercolor portraiture;
- Morris Hirshfield: fantasy painting;
- The Dentzel Family: carousel figure carving;
- J. Howard & Co.: weathervane production;
- John Blunt: portraiture;
- John Bellamy: marine carving;
- Julius Theodore Melchers: tobacconist figure carving;
- Aaron Mountz: animal carving;
- Durs Rudy: fraktur;
- Samuel Bentz: fraktur;
- Ruth Henshaw Bascom: watercolor portraiture;
- Hannah Davis: bandbox making;
- Rufus Hathaway: portraiture;
- John Bell: redware;
- John Brewster: portraiture;
- Miles Carpenter: outsider art;
- John Remmey: stoneware production;
- Rufus Porter: painting;
- Ann Butler: painted tinware decorator;
- Sheldon Peck: portraiture;
- Jacob Maentel: watercolor portraiture;
- Jurgan F. Huge: landscape painting;
- J.O.J. Frost: marine painting;
- Charles Hoffman: almshouse painting;
- Lem & Steve Ward: decoy production;
- Asahel Powers: portraiture;
- Deborah Goldsmith: portraiture;
- Sturtevant Hamblen: portraiture;
- Fritz Vogt: landscape drawings;
- Emily Eastman: watercolor portraiture;
- Mary Ann Willson: watercolor portraiture;
- Gus Wilson: watercolor portraiture;
- Hannah Otis: needlework;
- Joe Lincoln: decoy maker;
- Martin Ramirez: outsider art;
- Judith Scott: outsider art;
- Reuben Moulthrop: portraiture;

- John Reber: animal carving;
- Anthony Baecher: redware;
- Lanier Meaders: face vessels;
- John Flory: paint-decorated furniture;
- Henry Leach: weathervane patterns;
- Henry Young: fraktur;
- Zedekiah Belknap: portraiture;
- David Spinner: redware;
- Joshua Johnson: portraiture;
- William Jennys: portraiture;
- George Huebner: redware;
- Noah North: portraiture;
- Jonathan Fisher: portraiture;
- John Bradley: portraiture;
- M. W. Hopkins: portraiture;
- Elizabeth Perkins: portraiture;
- A. Ellis; portraiture;
- Christian Seltzer: paint-decorated furniture;
- John Kane: outsider art;
- Elder Henry Green: Shaker;
- Richard Brunton; portraiture;
- John Rassmussen: almshouse painting;
- John Dilley: decoy making;
- Frederick Myrick: scrimshaw;
- Elijah Pierce: outsider art;
- Minnie Evans: outsider art;
- Johannes Bard: fraktur;
- The Cross-Legged Angel Artist: fraktur;
- Heinrich Otto: fraktur;
- James Hampton: outsider art;
- William Hawkins: outsider art;
- Adolf Wolfli: outsider art.

12. Sources are as follows:

- Flayderman, E. Norman. *Scrimshaw & Scrimshanders, Whales & Whalemen*. N. Flayderman & Co., New Milford, CT, 1972.

- Kopp, Kate and Joel. *American Hooked and Sewn Rugs: Folk Art Underfoot*. EP Dutton, New York, 1975.

- Hollander, Stacy C., Wertkin, Gerard C., et al. *American Radiance: The Ralph Esmerian Gift to the American Folk Art.* Harry N. Abrams, New York, 2001.

- Orlofsky, Patsy and Myron. *Quilts in America.* Abbeville Press, New York, 1992 (reprint edition).

- Ring, Betty. *Girlhood Embroidery: American Samplers & Pictorial Needlework 1650–1850.* Alfred A. Knopf, New York, 1993.

- Fried, Frederick. *Artists in Wood: American Carvers of Cigar-Store Indians, Show Figures, and Circus Wagons.* Clarkson Potter, New York, 1970.

- Fales, Dean A. and Bishop, Robert. *American Painted Furniture, 1660–1880.* E.P. Dutton, New York, 1972.

- Watkins, Lura Woodside. *Early New England Potters & Their Wares.* Harvard University Press, Cambridge, MA, 1950.

- Kangas, Gene and Linda. *Decoys: A North American Survey.* Hillcrest Publications, Spanish Fork, UT, 1983.

- Rumford, Beatrix. *American Folk Paintings: Paintings and Drawings Other Than Portraits from the Abby Aldrich Rockefeller Folk Art Center.* New York Graphic Society, New York, 1988.

- Rumford, Beatrix. *American Folk Portraits: Paintings and Drawings from the Abby Aldrich Rockefeller Folk Art Center.* New York Graphic Society, New York, 1981.

- Webster, Donald Blake. *Decorated Stoneware Pottery of North America.* Charles E. Tuttle Company, Rutland, VT, 1971.

- Klamkin, Charles. *Weathervanes: the History, Design, and Manufacture of an American Folk Art.* Hawthorn Books Inc, New York, 1973.

13. Since most Americans couldn't read, trade signs indicated what business was conducted where.

14. Carved wooden Indians were used as trade signs for advertising purposes. The identification of Indians with the tobacco industry goes back to the late sixteenth and seventeenth centuries when Theodore de Bry published romanticized engravings of "Indians of South Florida."

H.O. Robinson Boot and Shoe Store Sign
c. 1880. Shield-shaped with separate wooden boots swinging on each side of the sign, black and gilt oil on board. Sign 24 1/2" H × 42 3/4" W; boots 14 3/4" H and 9" heel to toe. Photo courtesy David Wheatcroft Antiques

Whirligig of a Conductor
c. 1910, Zionsville, Ohio. Carved and painted wood, tin, leather and horsehair. 18 1/2" H Photo courtesy Olde Hope Antiques

Uncle Sam Whirligig
Made in Vermont in 1980 by Jonathon Fendelman. Polychrome wooden whirligig depicting Uncle Sam waving the American flag. 14" H
Photo courtesy of the owner

Native Americans introduced the crop to England's first settlers in Virginia; in the minds of seventeenth-century advertisers and trade sign makers back home in England, however, anyone who had anything to do with the tobacco industry in the New World was combined into one identity. Whether Native Americans who first grew tobacco, enslaved African-Americans who worked the tobacco fields, or Anglo-American settlers who exported the crop to England, all were "Indians." By the nineteenth century, this popular association was well established; though some trade signs in other forms (police officer, baseball player, fashionable lady, "Punch") do exist.

15. A weathervane shows the direction of the wind; a whirligig is a wind toy; a bannerette is a type of weathervane, usually in flattened flag-style form.

16. There are flat or full-bodied weathervanes constructed from wood, sheet iron, zinc, copper, or other metals made by individuals or factories from wooden molds. Some have hand-hammered details; some are gilded or painted.

17. Patina, form, condition, artistic merit, and construction. With respect to patina and condition, surfaces on weathervanes are easily fabricated. When examining the weathervane, consider how quickly the elements degrade any other object you may know—a wooden picnic table,

a lawn or beach chair, a park bench, the paint on a house—in 5 to 10 years, most common outdoor objects show damage from sun, wind, and rain, among other elements. Then consider if the weathervane you are examining makes sense for the age it purports to be—does it show evidence of decades of rain streaking down its sides? Does the rust follow a logical path and show history between whatever is rusting and whatever the rust touches? Most weathervanes with surface decoration, particularly delicate gilding, have been resurfaced at some point early in the object's life, legitimately and simply because of how they were used before they became considered art. Sheet metal weathervanes should not have a sharp edge if in fact they have been outdoors all their lives. Under usual circumstances, any wooden weathervane more than 25 years old and used outside should be starting to split or at least be on its way to falling apart.

18. In the age before photography, a painted portrait or portrait miniature was the only way to capture one's likeness or the likeness of a loved one. For sentimental reasons (the death of a child, for example) a portrait might be painted posthumously, or it might have been painted in celebration (a wedding portrait). As portraits became more affordable and America's exploding middle class more affluent, this particular type of painting, which had always been imbued with status symbol quality, was especially popular in documenting one's earthly successes and providing some kind of material legacy to the next generation. In a few instances, such as some portraits by late eighteenth-century Connecticut artist Ralph Earl, a portrait might include the landscape and buildings of the sitter's home in the background.

19. Simplification and minimization almost to the point of abstraction; directness; either a flatness indicating a lack of perspective or elements oddly juxtaposed suggesting more than one perspective; untrained or untutored style; the problems of the composition have not been solved by the artist; no definite light source, poor or no shading; bold color.

20. "Toleware" refers to European, specifically French, paint-decorated tin. In style and design, toleware is more so-

phisticated and urban than the American paint-decorated tin. Various means of decorating tin in America included piercing, punching, and freehand or stencil painting.

21. Among the common motifs seen in Pennsylvania German folk art are: the heart, tulip, dove, birds (distelfink, or goldfinch), parrot, peacock, geometric designs (pinwheel, hex, astragal).

22. Wood splint (willow, oak, ash), stems, twigs, roots and runners, barks, vines, grasses (rye), and rattan (Nantucket baskets).

23. Potato stamping, stenciling, brush painting, fruit and vegetable dyeing, freehand painting, weaving, and appliqué of other objects into the basket (such as porcupine quills).

24. A shirred rug is made from gathered strips of cloth sewn together and then sewn in a pattern onto a backing. A yarn-sewn rug is made of homespun worsted wool that is used in a sewn technique to create a pile surface by laying a flexible reed-like device on the backing and sewing over it with a needle. This technique was used from approximately 1800–1850. A hooked rug is made of strips of fabric, which are held under burlap backing. A hook is used to pull up, or hook, the fabric through the burlap to form the design.

25. Satin, French knot, cross-stitch, chain stitch, seed stitch, and whip stitch are the most common stitches seen in nineteenth-century needlework. Tent stitch and Queen's stitch appear in earlier needleworks. A satin stitch, or series of long, fine, parallel threads, gives a smooth, sheened "satin" appearance; French knot (achieved by wrapping the thread several times around the shaft of the needle before sending the needle through the canvas) gives a nubby, bumpy, textured stitch, often used in depicting sheep; cross-stitch (and double cross-stitch), the most common X-shaped stitch, important for marking textiles, is still in use today; a chain stitch is evenly spaced interlocking loops of thread; seed stitch, also called dot-stitch and speckling stitch, is a series of random, small, tight running stitches; a whip stitch is a series of slightly overlapping running stitches all done

on the same side of the fabric (also called stem-stitch, outline, crewel-stitch or stalk-stitch). Tent stitch and Queen's stitch are fancier canvaswork stitches. The former is a series of parallel stitches arranged diagonally across the intersection of the threads (also called petit point); the latter stitch produces a holed center.

26. Grain painting was done for a variety of practical and decorative reasons. First, it could be done to preserve the wood and prevent it from warping and cracking. Second, it was often done when the completed object was comprised of a variety of different stock woods, but the cabinetmaker wanted the final product to have a uniform appearance. Third, it could be done to make a less expensive wood look like a more exotic, imported hardwood in the masking dimness of available light forms in the nineteenth century. Finally, it was also done to enliven dark interiors and make household objects items more beautiful.

The brush was the basic tool used in decorating with paint. Amateurs and professionals alike, however, employed a wide variety of other implements—feathers, corn cobs, combs, sponges, crinkly paper, potatoes, hands, arms, fingers, fists, and even candle smoke, which produced a soft, hazy finish. Graining combs manufactured by various companies in England in the nineteenth century were largely replaced later by brushes. These combs were usually made of metal and came in all widths, thicknesses, and degrees of fineness. Some combs were made of leather for more flexibility and some even of ivory. Still later, to speed the work and to satisfy the greater demand for paint-decorated furniture, large rollers made of metal, wood, linoleum, or cut or etched rubber for printing a distinctive pattern were used. Handheld rollers were also produced for the home handyman.

Painting began with the application of a suitable base coat, usually a light color. After this was thoroughly dry, a contrasting graining color, a darker glaze in a fast drying paint, which sometimes included a combination of various paints with a touch of vinegar or beer, depending on the desired effect, was applied. That was allowed to set just enough so that it would not spread out when combed or become too dry to make graining difficult. While the glaze was still wet, the craftsperson using one or more tools completed the pattern.

27. Slip is a mixture of fine clay and water originally used as a cement to join parts of a hollowware vessel (such as a spout or handle) while still soft. It is used ornamentally by trailing one, two, or three lines of slip from a quilled container in a series of lines, squiggles, crosshatches, or even dots, similar to the way icing decorates a cake.

28. Scratching through the glaze to make a design in redware or stoneware pottery.

29. Scrimshaw is the art of carving or otherwise making useful or decorative articles by whalemen, sailors, or others involved in nautical pursuits. The basic material of scrimshaw is from the whale. Other materials may be taken from various sea life or areas visited by whale ships, as well as woods, metals, and other materials normally carried or used aboard ship. The parts of the whale that were used were the ivory teeth of odontal whales, the cartilaginous filtering mouth plates of baleen whales, and the bones of both.

The basic tool of the scrimshander was a jackknife or a sailor's needle, which was used to etch or incise a picture. The completed design was rubbed with ink, lamp black, or tobacco juice, so that the picture would be highly visible. All hands made much of the scrimshaw on shipboard to pass the time at sea during the height of the whaling industry, from 1820–1920.

30. Chalkware is plaster of Paris, which is poured into two-part molds and then decorated with brightly colored paint. To varying degrees, the resulting object is hollow, much like a chocolate Easter candy, with an open base as well. While often mistakenly associated with the Pennsylvania Germans, the forms in fact were often simplified imitations of English Staffordshire pottery made for a less affluent market throughout the eastern seaboard and inland. Chalkware was found in homes as often as Currier and Ives' prints were and was sold in America as early as the late eighteenth century to as late as the late nineteenth century. The material is highly fragile and

Theorem c. 1850, Northeastern United States. Oil on velvet depicting a basket of fruit with bird and butterfly accents. Approximately 14" H × 17" W Photo courtesy Raccoon Creek Antiques

Quaker Marking Sampler, 1825, Long Island, New York, by Freelove Townsend. Simplicity is the keynote of this Quaker sampler. 16" H × 18" W Photo courtesy M. Finkel & Daughter

even the most careful and delicate packing of a purchased object might end in powdery shards at its destination. Most surviving examples are mid-to-late nineteenth century; another group of carnival-inspired chalkware was made in the twentieth century.

Mourning Picture
c. 1830, New England, artist unknown. Watercolor on paper depicting a woman in mourning costume leaning on a tombstone, which is surrounded by stylized trees and architectural buildings, having the initials "E.R." inscribed on her scarf. Original frame.
$19^{1}/_{4}$"H × 24"W framed
Photo courtesy Frank & Barbara Pollack
American Antiques & Art

31. Review weathervane books for similar examples; review museum collections for similar examples; review auction house records for similar examples; consult a major folk art dealer, appraiser, or curator.

32. The sternboard is the decorative panel that adorns the back, or stern, of a ship. It can be a painted, bas-relief carving or painted without a carving. The figurehead is the ornamental wood carving, often in the shape of a human, that adorns the front, or bow, of a ship meant as its good luck symbol.

33. Ammi Phillips was a portrait painter who lived and worked in Western Connecticut, Massachusetts, and the bordering New York counties. He was thought to be

Album Quilt
c. 1840,
Wisconsin.
Pieced and
appliquéd
cotton.
76" H × 85" W
Private
collection;
Photo courtesy
Shelly Zegart

three artists until the research of Barbara and Lawrence Holdridge and Mary Black was presented as an exhibition in 1969 at the American Folk Art Museum in New York City. The three artists previously attributed to Phillips were the Border Limner, the Kent Limner and "Phillips" or "A. Phillips." The first period, known as the Border period, was from approximately 1812 to 1819 and was typified by painting in bulky and round form in pastel colors against a pale background. During the 1820s, Phillips painted more realistically, using light and shadow and a more somber palette. During the 1830s, he painted quickly and flatly using minimal highlights to suggest details and to separate the figures from their background. After 1840, elaborate costume details disappeared, and the figures became more straightforward. His likenesses grew similar to the prevailing photographic standard of the day. His "Kent Limner" identity resulted from a discernible quantity of his portraits descending in and being traceable to families in and around the Kent, Connecticut, area.

34. In the early nineteenth and later century, young women could be sent to a day or a boarding school where, for a modest fee, they would be taught reading, writing, arith-

metic, history, geography, grammar, composition, and needlework. Lessons in drawing and painting were also available. Theorem painting, samplers, cut paper, watercolor, and painting on furniture are also examples of artistic skills taught in these schools. They form the bulk of what is meant by schoolgirl, academy, or seminary art.

35. Log Cabin, Barn Raising, School House, Grandmother's Flower Garden, Wedding Ring, Double Wedding Ring, Baskets, Flower Baskets, Flying Geese, Star of Bethlehem, Sunshine and Shadow, Nine Patch, Album, Diamond in the Square, Bars, and Baby or Tumbling Blocks.

APPENDIX

GLOSSARY

alkaline glaze
alkaline glaze, an alternative to lead glazes, is produced with sodium and potassium oxides as modifiers. The alkaline glaze was accomplished by throwing salt in the kiln fire so it vaporized and reacted with silica and steam to produce "a salt glaze," usually on stoneware.

alligatoring
the separation of a surface treatment on its substrate; on finished furniture, this is often seen as a "scaly" crazing on the surface. On an oil painting, this is seen when the paint starts to flake and cup (also known as cracquelure).

Anna Pottery
stoneware made in the late nineteenth century by the Kirkpatrick Family of Anna, Illinois, usually using molded or encrusted animal and human forms or some variation thereof encircling the piece.

aniline dye
of the two major types of textile colorants, natural and chemical dyes, aniline dyes are a class of synthetic, organic dyes originally obtained from aniline coal tars in 1856 by William Perkins. Today the term is used with reference to any synthetic organic dyes and pigments, regardless of source, in contrast to natural dyes and synthetic inorganic pigments. Aniline dyes are classified according to their degree of brightness or their light fastness. Basic dyes are known for their extreme brightness as well as for their lack of color fastness.

applied
any separate decorative or functional element to a work that is not integral to its body but attached. Examples would be the spout or handle on a teapot, or a mid or base molding on case pieces of furniture.

appliqué
fabric cut into fanciful or representational shapes using one or a variety of colors and sewn onto a larger textile to create an overall pattern.

asphaltum

a composition of coal tar, lime, and sand used to create the waterproof surface and sealing ground on painted tinware, usually in a brown-eggplant color.

bandbox

lidded storage boxes in varying sizes and shapes, made from pasteboard and covered in wallpaper. The name "bandbox" originated in England between 1820–1850 to store men's neckbands and lace bands. Ladies used the boxes not only for their bonnets but also as portable storage compartments for hairpieces, dresses and jewelry, ribbons, and artificial flowers. The smaller boxes held gloves, handkerchiefs, powder, and sewing materials. Bandboxes, also called hatboxes, were usually lined with newspaper.

Bennington

Bennington Pottery and Porcelain was one of the most important ceramic factories of the mid-nineteenth century. Established in 1793 as an earthenware and brick manufacturer by John Norton in Bennington, Vermont, the company produced stoneware by 1815. The founder's sons, Luman and John, inherited this business in 1823 and it survived until 1894. In 1842–43, Luman's son, Julius Norton (1809–1861), established a factory making higher-quality wares with greater artistic aspirations with business partner Christopher Fenton (1806–1865). In 1849, Fenton patented a 'flint enamel' glaze, a mottled yellow, orange, blue, and brown combination of the ordinary tortoiseshell colored "Rockingham" glaze. This glaze was applied to both useful and ornamental wares, especially to jugs with handles in the form of greyhounds.

bleeding

the migration of one element of a work into another, usually onto the ground or receiving element of the same work. On furniture, this would be the rust and iron oxide of a nail or screw into the wood surrounding it; on a work on paper, this would be the watercolor or ink seeping into the body of the paper. Iron oxides in dark-colored thread also bled into the fabric ground on some needleworks.

brocade

imprecise term for a richly figured textile, especially one with a woven pattern in gold or silver thread. Similar in appearance on the obverse to a compound weave; distinguished on the reverse by the pattern seen in negative.

Bucher box
a specific group of paint-decorated boxes primarily made in the nineteenth century associated with the Pennsylvania Germans and usually distinguished by a dark background decorated with white, yellow, and red tulips. Made in three shapes—flat rectangular with hinged lid, rectangular with domed hinged lid, and an oval bandbox—named after the recipient of a box now in the collection of the Winterthur Museum.

calligraphy
during the early nineteenth century penmanship was an art. Platt Roger Spencer, a schoolmaster and expert penman, began the eponymous method of writing, through which skilled practitioners created fanciful pictorial art that included animals, trees, and houses. The alphabet was sometimes incorporated into the design.

candlewicking
a form of embroidery in which a white thread (traditionally, a candlewick) is stitched in an outline on a piece of muslin. Decorative knot stitches (colonial or French) primarily embellish these, as well as more simple stitches (backstitch, stem stitch, chain stitch, satin stitch). The worked textile is then washed in hot water to shrink the fabric around the stitches. This highlights the raised effect of the work. At a distance, candlewicking appears similar to other stuffed work, such as trapunto, but the raised part of the pattern is above the fabric ground, not underneath, which makes it similar to chenille.

carved
any form or decorative element produced by incision or removal with a blade.

cast
any form or decorative element produced by pouring a liquid medium into a negative mold of the final form, such as cast iron or chalkware.

chalkware
plaster of Paris molded in imitation of Staffordshire pottery, usually brightly painted.

cobalt decoration

cobalt, one of the strongest coloring oxides used in pottery, creates a dark, dense royal blue in most cases. It is typically seen in animal or floral motifs on American stoneware pottery.

compound weave

any type of woven structure that involves more than two sets of elements—such as one (or more) warp sets, plus two (or more) weft sets, which are manipulated through different paths to create a pattern; see *warp* and *weft*.

copper

reddish colored malleable and ductile base metal usually used in production as an alloy.

cotton

white-to-yellowish fiber made from the blossom of several species of the plant of the mallow family; used especially for making textiles, cords, and padding.

cracquelure

see *alligatoring*.

crazing

a fine network of small cracks. See *alligatoring*.

crazy quilt

late nineteenth-century quilt pattern using a mix of irregularly shaped fabrics pieced in a random, almost scattered shard arrangement; usually executed in silk, velvet, and satin, but other fabrics are also used, often with embroidery-embellished seams or appliquéd or embroidered mementos; sometimes with fan-shaped piecing punctuating the overall pattern. Crazy quilts were made into the twentieth century.

crib quilt

smaller-sized quilt designed to fit an infant's bed.

crystalline decoration

a type of decoration, usually seen on nineteenth-century American paint-decorated tinware in which an etching process produces a metallic, almost engine-turned, effect on the tinware, which is then painted.

decoupage
in the nineteenth century, a technique for decorating surfaces with paper cutouts, or other flat material, over which a finish is applied. Joseph Long Lehn (1798–1892) was one artist whose production was often decorated with decoupage.

double woven
a textile woven with two warps and two wefts.

end out
an addition to an original, often done during restoration, to make up a missing portion on a work of art. Examples include a furniture leg onto which an addition has been made to level it or a work on paper onto which a small piece has been added to repair a torn corner.

figurehead
the decorative carving on a ship's bow, often depicting a human, used as a good-luck symbol for the ship.

finish
the sealing and protective coating on furniture as well as fabrics.

fireboard
painting on wooden panel executed to the measurements of the fireplace and used during the summer to block the fireplace opening and to prevent drafts.

fire bucket
buckets used by individual households, before the advent of fire departments, to assist in putting out fires. Usually made of leather that has been painted in some decorative way, often identifying the name of the private fire society that would be responsible for putting out the fire.

flaking
the cracking and lifting of oil pigment off canvas.

foxing
stains, specks, spots, and blotches in paper usually occurring in machine-made paper of the late eighteenth, nineteenth, and twentieth centuries. The cause or causes of foxing are not completely known but are probably due to fungi, acid, or oxide in nature. Foxing can also be seen on fabrics.

fraktur

the literal translation is broken or "fractured" writing; this type of fancy lettering was done on a variety of decorated documents, birth and baptismal certificates; house blessings; bookplates; rewards of merit in watercolor on paper with ink, usually by the Pennsylvania Germans, but also seen in German communities in the American South. Henry Chapman Mercer first put the word into use in the late 1890s.

French knot

a fancy needlework stitch to indicate a nubby texture, such as a sheep's coat in a pictorial work. Done by wrapping the thread several times around the shaft of the needle before sending the needle through the canvas to secure the stitch.

Grenfell

hooked rugs and mats made by residents of northern Newfoundland and Labrador in a tightly hooked style very similar to needlepoint. Their production was promoted by Dr. Wilfred Grenfell as a cottage industry to supplement the income of the local fishing families with its peak from the 1920s through the 1940s.

grisaille

painting in various shades of gray and white, usually in trompe l'oeil to imitate carved stone; most often associated in America with kasten, cupboards, or armoires made in the Hudson River Valley.

grotesque jug

a stoneware or redware pottery vessel in the form of a human face, sometimes called a face jug, used most often for decorative purposes.

Hadley chest

made in the Hadley, Massachusetts area. In the late seventeenth and early eighteenth centuries, these chests are distinguished for their exuberant floral carving. They were orginally paint-decorated.

hatbox

usually made from pasteboard and covered in wallpaper, and seen in as many shapes as hats were made. Among the most famous of American hatbox makers is Hannah Davis of Jaffrey, New Hampshire. See *bandbox*.

hooked rug

a type of floor covering most popular in the nineteenth and twentieth centuries, but also seen in bed coverings of the eighteenth century. The background material is linen or burlap, and the pile is formed of narrow strips of wool or cotton rags drawn up from the ground fabric by means of a hook to form loops.

inpaint

an area of any painted object, whether canvas or furniture, where the original paint has been filled in or restored.

iron

a lustrous, silvery, soft base metal that rusts when exposed to moist air. Often used in combination with other metals as an alloy to make various objects, either cast or wrought, and used with other substances to make other materials; see *iron oxide* and *socking gall*.

iron oxide

in pottery, a colorant that, when combined with the right glaze and firing, can produce greens, browns, blacks, yellows, oranges, subtle blues, and grays.

Jacquard

a means of weaving fabric invented by Joseph-Marie Jacquard (1752–1834) of Lyon, France, in which complex patterns could be hand-loomed by one weaver.

japanning

a method of decorating wood using gesso to form a design, then using paint and lacquer over it; also, a type of painting usually done in a style evoking Asian art, most commonly on a black background.

kas; kasten

the Dutch term for a portable closet; also called armoire (French) or schrank (German). Usually associated with New York production.

laminate

a material composed of thin layers of the same or alternating materials, usually of wood, sealed together.

limner
painter, usually refers to an itinerant painter who worked in a naive style.

linen
general name for a textile woven from the spun fiber of the flax plant.

molded
any object whose form is made by imposing a shape on the essential medium, whether the material is pressed against a positive (drape molded pottery, some weathervanes), or poured into a negative (chalkware).

Mount Lebanon
one of several communal settlements established by the Shakers in New York State, Mount Lebanon was founded in 1787.

over mantel painting
usually depicting a landscape or townscape, done on a wooden panel to be installed over a fireplace.

overshot
overshot weaving designs are created by weft threads that skip over groups of warp threads. The overshot pattern thread is usually of a thicker yarn than the ground tabby weft. Pattern blocks are created using a twill treadling, and unit blocks can be done in any sequence any number of times.

piece
putting together a whole from parts; in quilting, the individual components of an overall design may be created by joining, or "piecing" fabric fragments.

plain weave
the simplest fabric weave comprised of one warp and one weft, each equally passed over the other. Also called "tabby weave."

punch decoration
a technique to embellish furniture, metal, and ceramics by which a pattern is impressed, or punched, into the object body.

quilt top
the unquilted, but completed pattern side of a quilt.

raking light
strong light from one source shone across a surface to create shadows that reveal surface inconsistencies.

redware
a brittle, friable earthenware made from red clay and fired at a low temperature. This type of pottery must be glazed to hold water.

reverse appliqué
in quilting, shapes made in the negative and sewn onto a ground in the same way appliqué is done.

Rockingham glaze
tortoise shell–colored glaze in brown and yellow used on a variety of functional pieces of pottery and created with manganese brown glaze dripped onto the piece at the second firing. This gives the piece a mottled effect. The glaze is named for Charles Watson-Wentworth Rockingham, the second marquis of Rockingham, who led the group known as the Rockingham Whigs to oppose Britain's war against its colonists in North America.

Sabbath Day Lake
one of several communal settlements established by the Shakers in Maine. The Sabbath day Lake Community was founded in 1783. In less than a year, nearly two hundred people had gathered together in this place that previously had only been the home of some five farming families.

salt glaze
see *alkaline glaze*.

sampler
common term for a girl's needlework in which a "sampling" of the stitches she knew were executed, often in a fancy, graphic, or pictorial format.

Santos
Mexican- and Spanish-influenced Southwestern carved religious figures.

satin stitch
a type of fancy needlework stitch in which parallel lines of thread, usually silk, were tightly placed over a relatively small surface area both to fill in a given color and create a smooth, shiny appearance to the silk picture.

satin weave
fabric weave in which the weft threads are woven over three or more warp threads, creating a soft, lustrous textile; most commonly seen with silk. The fabric we generally call "satin" is actually a satin-woven silk. When satin is woven in cotton, it is called 'sateen.'

scherenschnitte
cut paper designs or pictures, also called cutwork, usually associated with Pennsylvania German artists.

screening varnish
a heavy layer of varnish (shellac) placed on a painted surface, often to obscure a repair or area of inpaint.

scrimshaw
incised design filled with ink or lamp black and executed on a whale's tooth, baleen, or bone, usually made by seamen during the nineteenth century.

seed stitch
also called dot stitch and speckling stitch, a seed stitch is a series of random, small, tight-running stitches intended to look like small dots, dashes or, as the name suggests, seeds on a needlework ground. This stitch is commonly seen in nineteenth-century pictorial needlework.

seminary work
schoolboy or schoolgirl art such as samplers, paintings, penmanship or calligraphy drawings, and theorems.

sewn rug
homespun worsted wool that is used in a sewn technique to create a pile surface by laying a flexible reed-like device on the backing and sewing over it with a needle.

sgraffito
scratching through the glaze of redware or stoneware pottery to create a design.

Shenandoah pottery

slip-covered redware pottery with multicolored glazes, often associated with the output of the Bell Potteries at Winchester and Strasburg, Virginia, and Waynesboro, Pennsylvania. The Bell Potteries produced wares between 1835–1880.

shirred rug

a shirred rug is made of gathered strips of cloth sewn together and then sewn in a pattern onto a backing.

socking gall

the damaging effect of iron gall ink on paper. Inks manufactured from iron salts and gallotannic acid are called iron gall inks. Gallotannic acid is found in oak and other galls. Iron gall inks were used extensively for manuscripts. Since these inks contain iron and acid, which both attack paper, they can be very damaging. For example, iron gall ink has been known to dissolve paper completely; many fraktur survive with their inscribed portions completely destroyed and appearing now almost to be cut outs because the acid from the ink has eaten through the paper.

stencil decoration

any paint decoration produced by means of a template precut with a pattern.

sternboard

the decoratively carved or painted board that embellishes the rear, or stern, of a boat.

stoneware

a highly fired feldspathic clay mixed with fusible stone to produce a vitrified, durable body capable of holding liquid even when not glazed.

strainer

in picture framing, a wooden auxiliary support made up of a minimum of four members on which a canvas is stretched. It differs from a stretcher in that the corners are not adjustable.

stretcher

in picture framing, a wooden auxiliary support made up of a minimum of four members on which a canvas is stretched. It has expandable corners so that its dimensions can be slightly increased when necessary.

stretcher wedges
in painting frames, small, wedge-shaped sections of wood are inserted in the corners of stretchers and enable the dimensions of the stretcher to be increased when they are tapped in.

stuffwork
technique of decorating textiles in which a motif is defined by a running stitch and then stuffed, usually with batting, to create a raised effect. Trapunto is an example of stuffwork or stuffed work.

synthetics
usually refers to textiles and pigments (paints and dyes) or anything produced by combining elements, materials, or entities into a new whole. Synthetics can be composed of organic or inorganic materials but are distinguished from natural things; they are artificial.

tent stitch
a series of parallel stitches arranged diagonally across the intersection of the threads. This stitch is also called petit point.

theorem
a type of painting popularized in the nineteenth century that usually depicts a still life, often flowers and/or fruit. Theorems are created with a variety of stencils using watercolor on either velvet or paper.

thrown
the means by which pottery is built up on a wheel. Clay is "thrown" onto a turning wheel; as the wheel turns, the potter grows and shapes the sides.

tinware
any decorative tin object embellished by piercing, punching or painting.

tramp art
chip-carved and layered fruit, vegetable, or cigar boxes remade into boxes, frames, furniture, and other decorative art objects.

trapunto
raised and stuffed design on a quilt or other textile.

trompe l'oeil
literally to 'trick the eye' into believing that what is depicted is real; realistic painting.

turned
any furniture part whose decoration is achieved on a lathe through the application of variously shaped bits. Examples would be the legs on a table or chair, the stiles on a slat-back chair, the applied split-spindle decoration on a frame.

twill weave
a fabric weave by which the weft threads cover two or three warp threads at a time, with the amount covered by the weft threads moving systematically over one or more warp threads at a time so as to produce a diagonal appearance to the fabric. Common examples in current everyday use include the cotton twill of khaki pants and blue jeans.

vegetable dye
of the two major types of textile colorants, natural and chemical dyes, vegetable dyes come from plant extractions such as indigo, henna, madder, and walnut. Other natural dyes include animal dyes (cochineal) and mineral dyes (ocher). Some textiles, such as cotton, require a mordant (fixative) to absorb the color. Dyes that require a mordant are called adjective dyes; dyes that do not require a mordant to be absorbed are called substantive dyes.

velvet (cut and looped)
a silk or cotton textile with a pile produced by inserting rods onto the warp during weaving to raise the warp into even loops. If the loops are cut, the fabric is called a *cut velvet*; if the loops remain, it is an *uncut velvet*. It is called *solid* if the ground is entirely covered with pile, *voided* when areas of ground are left free of pile. Patterns may be made by cutting some areas of pile and leaving others uncut.

Waldoboro rugs
hooked rugs from Waldoboro, Maine, noted for their raised or stuffed appearance similar to trapunto work in a quilt. They were popular from the 1880s to the 1930s.

wax relining

an older method of relining a painting in which a new canvas is adhered to the original canvas by means of a medial layer of wax. The old and new canvases are joined by heat pressing, which melts the wax and seals the two canvases together.

whale end shelf

a type of hanging shelf popular in the mid-nineteenth century whose sides, in which the shelves are secured, resemble in profile the shape of a sperm whale.

whitework

popular in the early nineteenth century, whitework was embroidery in white thread on a white ground, often incorporating eyelets into the pattern. A variety of different types of whitework exists including candlewicking, broderie Anglaise, and Ayshire needlework. The type of whitework is usually predicated on the fineness or coarseness of the thread and ground fabric.

wool

the soft coat of a sheep or other ungulate animal that is then washed, dried, carded, or combed before being woven into threads and fabrics.

wrigglework

a means of decorating metals and pottery by rocking a gouge or engraving a pattern of wormlike zigzag lines onto the surface.

wrought

a metal object whose shape is achieved through beating or hammering as opposed to casting. This term also refers to needlework and the act of creating a stitch.

zinc

a hard, brittle bluish type of metal not used in America until the mid-nineteenth century and valued for its particularly weather-resistant qualities as well as its ability to be cast in even the most detailed and delicate molds.

BIBLIOGRAPHY

The following online merchants may be able to provide additional titles or out-of-print books from the core list of essential reading below.

www.alibris.com
www.abebooks.com
www.amazon.com
www.bn.com
www.bookfinder.com

In addition the following book dealers can help you build a library. They include:

Joslin Hall Rare Books
Elizabeth & Forrest Proper
P.O. Box 516
Concord, MA 01742
Phone: 978-371-3101
Fax: 978-371-6445
Web site: www.joslinhall.com

Krause Publications
700 E. State St.
Iola, WI 54990-0001
Phone: 715-445-2214 or
715-445-5087
Fax: 800-334-7165

Mad Anthony Books
Linda Roggow
Carole Chenevert
Phone: 800-743-5404
E-mail: books@madanthony.com
Web site:
www.madanthonybooks.com

The Reference Rack
Box 445C
Orefield, PA 18069
Phone: 800-722-7279
Fax: 610-706-0229

F. Russack Books Inc.
Rick Russack
20 Beach Plain Road
Danville, NH 03819
Phone and Fax: 603-642-7718
Web site:
www.BooksAboutAntiques.com

Schiffer Publishing
Tina Skinner
Phone: 610-593-1777
Fax: 610-593-2002
E-mail: schifferbk@aol.com
Web site: www.schifferbooks.com

Two sources for old auction catalogs are:

Andy Rose
The Catalog Kid
P. O. Box 2194
Ocean, NJ 07712
Phone: 800-258-2056
Fax: 732-502-9156
Web site: www.catalogkid.com

Jeffrey Eger
42 Blackberry Lane
Morristown, NJ 07960
Phone: 973-455-1843
Fax: 973-455-0186
Web site: www.jeffreyeger.com

The following is a list of must-read books to get you started on your American folk art journey! The list is more heavily weighted toward mixed media publications so as to provide a visual and object-based definition of American folk art. Whether building your own or supporting a local institution, access to a good library is critical to learning about American folk art. The pictures also make it fun! When visiting antique shows, always be sure to stop by the bookseller's booth—some of these titles are out of print, and you will learn of other books that are also hard to find.

General (including collections and mixed media anthologies)

Bishop, Robert, Lipman, Jean and Warren, Elizabeth. *Five-Star Folk Art: One Hundred American Masterpieces.* Harry N. Abrams, New York, 1990. Identifying quality is the core goal of this book. By examining portraits, textiles, sculpture, furniture, all made over a span of 200 years and from a variety of public and private collections, this book discusses the specific features that make each object a masterpiece. Also included is general information on American Folk Art and biographical details of specific artists.

Earnest, Adele. *Folk Art in America.* Schiffer Publishing, Exton, PA, 1984. This more personal account of American folk art from a founding member of the American Folk Art Museum in New York City outlines masterpieces of the subject, describes the history of its collecting popularity in America and identifies several early collectors whose acquisitions not only secured a place for American folk art in the art market but provided a canon for later collectors.

Garvan, Beatrice B. *The Pennsylvania German Collection.* Philadelphia: The Philadelphia Museum of Art, 1982. Part of a series of "Handbooks in American Art," *The Pennsylvania German Collection* remains the most comprehensive 'field guide' to Pennsylvania German folk art. Comprised of 337 pages of black and white thumbnail photographs of material in the museum's collection, with catalog descriptions of each, the book continues with well-researched biographical information on every known artist included, translations of German-American texts and a full bibliography for further research.

Hartigan, Lynda Roscoe, et al. *Made with Passion: The Hemphill Folk Art Collection in the National Museum of American Art.* Smithsonian Institution Press, Washington, D.C., 1990. *Made with Passion* is the catalog of the 1986 National Museum of American Art's exhibition of author and founding American Folk Art Museum curator Herbert Waide Hemphill, Jr.'s personal collection, which the NMA purchased. The catalog of almost 200 objects encompasses both traditional and alternative examples of American folk art with detailed and illustrated entries on each object.

Hemphill, Herbert W., Jr. and Weissman, Julia. *Twentieth Century American Folk Art & Artists.* EP Dutton, New York, 1974. This book, covering 145 contemporary folk artists, followed the groundbreaking Fall 1970 exhibition of the same name at the American Folk Art Museum, which was the first curated exhibition on the subject. The book includes 100 color and 200 black and white illustrations as well as a complete artist index.

Hollander, Stacy C., Wertkin, Gerard C., et al. *American Radiance: The Ralph Esmerian Gift to the American Folk Art Museum.* Harry N. Abrams, New York, 2001. This book is a celebration of American folk art, its premier museum and the exceptional eye of one of its benefactors. Focusing primarily on traditional American folk art in almost all media and with a special emphasis on Pennsylvania German folk art, this book chronicles in meticulous detail the 341 objects comprising Esmerian's gift to the museum in almost 800 illustrations, half of which are in color. Additional contributions from over 12 specialists in the American folk art field make this book one of the most important titles on the subject.

Hollander, Stacy C., Anderson, Brooke Davis, et al. *American Anthem: Masterworks from the American Folk Art Museum.* Harry N. Abrams, New York, 2002. Following the publication of *American Radiance, American Anthem* applies the same meticulous scholarship and reassessment to a representative group of objects from the American Folk Art Museum's permanent collection. *American Anthem* covers the full range of the museum's holdings, from traditional American folk art to more contemporary works by an international group of artists. The latter is an especially important inclusion because it charts the map for future considerations of American folk art and underscores that folk are still making art in the naive tradition.

Hornung, Clarence P. *Treasury of American Design and Antiques: A Pictorial Survey of Popular Folk Arts Based upon Watercolor Renderings in the Index of American Design, at the National Gallery of Art.* Abradale Press, New York, 1997. With almost 3,000 illustrations, 800 in color, this book is a visual definition of American folk art. Originally published in the 1930s through the Works Progress Administration's Federal Art Project, this updated edition of the *Index of American Design* not only follows American design from its earliest colonial points to later factory production, but the new version also tracks down the location and interim history of many of the original objects included in Hornung's survey.

Lipman, Jean and Winchester, Alice. *The Flowering of American Folk Art: 1776–1876.* Viking Press, New York, 1974. *The Flowering of American Folk Art* is the catalogue accompanying the 1974 traveling exhibition spearheaded by the Whitney Museum of American Art. With its contents divided into four essential categories of art (painting, sculpture, architectural art, furniture and decorative arts), the book is a definitive account of American folk art and its artists during the United States' first century.

Little, Nina Fletcher. *Little by Little: Six Decades of Collecting American Decorative Arts.* E.P. Dutton, Inc., New York, 1984. In this book, pioneer New England folk art and decorative arts scholar, collector and benefactress Nina Fletcher Little recounts self-effacingly and with an extraordinary depth of knowledge how she and her husband, Bertram K. Little, formed one of New England's premier collections of 17th to 19th century Americana. The Littles were among the great collectors of the 20th century, with many of their possessions going to the Society for the Preservation of New England Antiquities on their death. The remainder of the items comprised one of the most important two-part auctions of the 20th century.

Yelen, Alice. *Passionate Visions of the American South Self-Taught Artists from 1940 to the Present*. University Press of Mississippi, Jackson, 1994. This catalog accompanies the eponymous 1993 exhibition held at the New Orleans Museum of Art. Featuring almost 300 works of art by approximately eighty Southern artists, the catalog includes biographical information and is well illustrated.

Sculpture (including weathervanes, carousel animals, and cigar store figures)

Bishop, Robert. *American Folk Sculpture* , E.P. Dutton, Inc., New York, 1974. This book is a comprehensive study of the subject divided into twenty-three category chapters. With over 600 black and white and 100 color illustrations, this book provides an important visual record of traditional and contemporary American folk sculpture and is considered a seminal title on the subject.

Bishop, Robert and Coblentz, Patricia. *Gallery of American Weathervanes and Whirligigs*. E.P. Dutton, New York, 1981. This book provides an overview on the subject, including descriptions of the major weathervane manufacturers and

distinctive examples of American whirligigs and wind toys.

Dinger, Charlotte. *Art of the Carousel*. Carousel Art, Green Village, NJ, 1984. Written by one of the preeminent carousel experts and collectors, and profusely illustrated, *Art of the Carousel* is the definitive work on the subject.

Flayderman, E. Norman. *Scrimshaw & Scrimshanders, Whales & Whalemen*. N. Flayderman & Co., New Milford, CT 1972. Written by noted collector, Norman Flayderman, this well illustrated book is considered one of the best and most complete on the subject.

Fried, Frederick. *Artists in Wood: American Carvers of Cigar-Store Indians, Show Figures, and Circus Wagons*. Clarkson Potter, New York, 1970. This well illustrated book, containing almost 30 color and over 200 black and white images, provides biographical information on thirty-seven different carvers and their shops, including period photographs of some and four reprints of specific shop catalogs.

Kangas, Gene and Linda. *Decoys: A North American Survey*. Hillcrest Publications, Spanish Fork, UT, 1983. This well-written, profusely illustrated and easy-to-read book by wood-turner and artist, Gene Kangas and his wife, remains one of the primary texts on the subject.

Klamkin, Charles. *Weathervanes: The History, Design, and Manufacture of an American Folk Art*. Hawthorn Books Inc, New York, 1973. This book is an excellent resource on the subject from its earliest hand wrought wood and sheet iron examples to later molded industrial manufacture.

Lipman, Jean. *American Folk Art in Wood, Metal and Stone*. Dover Publications, Mineola, NY, 1972. This reprint of the 1948 classic written by one of the doyennes of the field, American folk art collector Jean Lipman, includes 183 illustrations and focuses primarily on carved and painted American folk sculpture from the 18th to the end of the 19th centuries.

Manns, William and Shank, Peggy, et al. *Painted Ponies: American Carousel Art*. Zon International Publishing Company, Santa Fe, NM, 1987. With over 650 color photographs, this book provides readers with an excellent sampling of the best of American carousel art from private collections and operating parks. The text also includes directories, charts and guides for more seriously interested readers.

Maresca, Frank and Ricco, Roger, et al. *American Vernacular New Discoveries in Folk, Self-Taught and Outsider Sculpture*. Bullfinch Press, New York, 2002. With contributions from Margit Rowell and Joseph Jacobs, this book, written by Lyle Rexer, reassesses the traditional story on American folk sculpture and reevaluates its place within the art historical mainstream. With its lavishly illustrated text, the book introduces new ways of considering and identifying contemporary American folk sculpture.

Weedon, Geoff and Ward, Richard. *Fairground Art: the Art Forms of Traveling Fairs, Carousels and Carnival Midways*. Abbeville Press/Whitemouse Editions, London, 1981. This well-illustrated book provides an international overview of carved and paint-decorated entertainment sculpture as it evolved in

England, America, Germany, France, Belgium and Holland.

Furniture (including painted furniture and tramp art)

Fabian, Monroe. *Pennsylvania German Decorated Chest*. Main Street Books, New York, 1978. Fabian's book is essential reference material for this group of highly popular and prized paint-decorated furniture and presents design traditions distinct to each county of southeastern Pennsylvania. Well illustrated with color (48) and black and white (250) photographs, the book is also out of print and quite expensive.

Fales, Dean A. and Bishop, Robert. *American Painted Furniture, 1660-1880*. E.P. Dutton, New York, 1972. This essential text examines the prominent traditions in American paint-decorated furniture from its earliest colonial expressions to late Victorian examples. The book is profusely illustrated with almost 150 color plates and over 400 black and white photographs.

Fendelman, Helaine and Taylor, Jonathan. *Tramp Art: A Folk Art Phenomenon*. Stewart, Tabori & Chang, New York, 1999. Written by collector, scholar, teacher, appraiser, and author, Helaine Fendelman, and photographer Jonathan Taylor, *Tramp Art* dispels many of the myths and much of the misinformation surrounding this early 20th century folk carving and places it within the tradition of art forms passed from one generation to the next. Once comparatively ignored by collectors, tramp art has more recently become highly desirable in the marketplace. The extensive color illustrations provided in this book, coupled with its comprehensive examination of the subject, make this an important title for anyone interested in this material.

Decorative Arts (including boxes, baskets, tin, iron and treen)

Coffin, Margaret. *The History and Folklore of American Country Tinware, 1700–1900*. Thomas Nelson, Camden, NJ, 1968. This well written and illustrated text discusses leading tinware manufacturers in the 18th and 19th centuries as well as the marks identifying old tin.

Kauffman, Henry J. *Early American Ironware*. Weathervane Books, New York, 1966. This small, well illustrated book offers a good introduction to American cast and wrought iron for collectors.

Ketchum, William C. *American Basketry and Woodenware A Collector's Guide*. MacMillan Publishing Company, New York, 1974. As the title says, this book is a field guide for collectors on what to look for in two categories where condition is everything.

Lasansky, Jeannette. *To Cut, Piece and Solder*. Pennsylvania State University Press, Harrisburg, 1982. This thin text is laden with technical information and illustrations on undecorated American tin.

Little, Nina Fletcher. *Neat and Tidy: Boxes and Their Contents Used in Early American Households*. E.P. Dutton, Inc., New York, 1983. Although focused on a narrow group of material (boxes), this book is nonetheless a classic for identifying different makers, artists, and uses.

Philbrook Museum of Art, and Wyckoff, Lydia L. ed. *Woven Worlds:* *Baskets from the Clark Field Collection*. University of New Mexico Press, Santa Fe, 2001. This exhibition catalog documents over 1,000 baskets made by over 250 Native American peoples ranging from the Southeast, California, the Arctic and Sub-Arctic, and the Eastern Woodlands. This book is a comprehensive examination of the subject.

Schiffer, Herbert, Peter and Nancy. *Antique Iron: A Survey of American and English Forms, 15th Century through 1850*. Schiffer Publishing, Exton, PA, 1979. This book, profusely illustrated with almost 1,000 photographs, is a basic survey of American and English architectural hardware, lighting devices, andirons, kitchen tools and fireplace equipment.

Shaw, Robert and Burris, Ken. *American Baskets: A Cultural History of a Traditional Domestic Art*. Clarkson Potter, New York, 2000. This book is a basic and thorough introduction to the subject and an essential for any collector. Combining analyses of culture, geography and environment, Shaw produces an overall work addressing Native American traditions, Anglo-American and other European immigrant traditions, African-American forms as well as distinct groups within America such as the Shakers.

Teleki, Gloria Roth. *The Baskets of Rural America*. EP Dutton, New York, 1975. This well illustrated scholarly survey is a guide to identifying different baskets by region or tribe, including Native American, New England, Shaker, Nantucket, Pennsylvania, Appalachian, Midwest, coastal American South and African-American among others. Also discussed are for whom the baskets were made, how they were made, and for what they were originally used.

Toller, Jane. *Treen and Other Turned Woodware for Collectors*. David and Charles, 1975. Written by a treenware dealer, this brief book, with almost 40 black and white illustrations, guides collectors in their quest.

Pottery (including redware and stoneware)

Bivins, John and Rauschenburg, Bradford L. *The Moravian Potters in North Carolina*. University of North Carolina Press, Winston-Salem, 1972. This book is one of the seminal texts identifying North Carolina's significant Moravian pottery tradition. Bivins and Rauschenburg also distinguish their subject from its similar Pennsylvania counterparts.

Watkins, Lura Woodside. *Early New England Potters & Their Wares*. Harvard University Press, Cambridge, MA, 1950. With ample black and white illustrations, this book remains a standard resource on New England pottery as it addresses the subject beyond Bennington.

Webster, Donald Blake. *Decorated Stoneware Pottery of North America*. Charles E. Tuttle Company, Rutland, VT, 1971. This book is well illustrated in black and white and provides excellent details on technique and manufacturers.

Zusy, Catherine. *Norton Stoneware and American Redware in the Bennington Museum Collection*. Bennington Museum, Bennington, VT, 1991. This slim volume covers the most commonly associated pottery forms in New England.

Painting (including portraits, landscapes, watercolor)

Black, Mary. *American Folk Painting*. Clarkson Potter, New York, 1966. This profusely illustrated book by one of the field's premier curators is an excellent introduction to the subject.

Chotner, Deborah. *American Naive Watercolors and Drawings*. National Gallery of Art, Washington, DC, 1984. This exhibition catalog shows the museum's holdings of American folk art works on paper and includes a checklist of artists.

Emans, Charlotte M. and D'Ambrosio, Paul S. *Folk Art's Many Faces: Portraits in the New York State Historical Association*. New York State Historical Association, Cooperstown, NY, 1987. With extensive color illustrations of documented works attending each artist's biography, this book is an important examination of portraiture in pre-industrial America, all culled from works within the collection of the New York State Historical Association.

Karolik, M. & M. *M. & M. Karolik Collection of American Watercolors & Drawings 1800 -1875* (Two volumes). Museum of Fine Arts, Boston, 1962. These books document and illustrate the artists and works in one of the finest museum collections of American art.

Rumford, Beatrix. *American Folk Paintings: Paintings and Drawings Other Than Portraits from the Abby Aldrich Rockefeller Folk Art Center*. New York Graphic Society, New York, 1988. This well-researched book covers works on canvas, works on paper from landscape to still life, family records, theorem and schoolgirl art. As the title says, everything but portraits is shown. Nearly 400 works of art are included along with fully illustrated entries on each work from the museum's collection.

Rumford, Beatrix. *American Folk Portraits: Paintings and Drawings from the Abby Aldrich Rockefeller Folk Art Center*. New York Graphic Society, New York, 1981. Like its companion volume published in 1988, this book uses the museum's extensive collection of American folk portraits to discuss specific artists, identify their styles and discuss works by as yet then unidentified artists in AARFAC's collection as well. The book well illustrates and documents each portrait.

Textiles (including quilts, coverlets, hooked rugs and needlework samplers)

Anderson, Clarita S. and Hurst, Ronald L. *American Coverlets and Their Weavers: Coverlets from the Collection of Foster and Muriel McCarl*. Ohio State University Press, Columbus, Ohio, 2002. This latest publication on the subject accompanies the exhibition of the McCarl Collection at the Abby Aldrich Rockefeller Folk Art Museum at Colonial Williamsburg. The collection focuses predominantly on Mid-Atlantic jacquard woven coverlets from the first half of the 19th century. Generously illustrated, including many full-page images with close-up details, this book offers the most recent biographical information on over 700 known weavers.

Huber, Stephen and Carol. *Miller's Treasure or Not? How to Compare and Value Samplers*. Miller's Publications, London, 2002. This well illustrated book is an excellent concise guide to collectors in what to look for in American needlework, and how to assess quality, condition and authenticity. The text includes resources for the care and maintenance of antique textiles as well.

Kopp, Kate and Joel. *American Hooked and Sewn Rugs Folk Art Underfoot*. EP Dutton, New York, 1975. This concise book by dealers Kate and Joel Kopp identifies a variety of different materials, makers and pattern designers, as well as superlative single effort examples. The text includes technical information as well.

Orlofsky, Patsy and Myron. *Quilts in America*. Abbeville Press, New York, 1992 (reprint edition). Written by textile expert and conservator, Patsy Orlofsky, with prior contributions from her now deceased husband, Myron, this book chronicles the evolution of the quilt in America from its earliest, simple patterns to the explosion in quilt making design of the 19th century and includes some discussion of today's art quilt as well. This book includes excellent technical information regarding fabrics, patterns and quilting techniques.

Ring, Betty. *Girlhood Embroidery: American Samplers & Pictorial Needlework 1650-1850*. Alfred A. Knopf, New York, 1993. Covering the prime of American needlework arts in the original thirteen colonies, this two-volume book divides the subject into geographic areas and then examines the evolution of American needlework through each state or region, chronologically. Written by collector and noted author Betty Ring, *Girlhood Embroidery* is profusely illustrated and considered one of the most comprehensive and important scholarly publications on American needlework.

Shein, Joseph D. and Zongor, Melinda. *Coverlets and the Spirit of America: The Shein Coverlets*. Schiffer Publishing, Exton, PA, 2002. The beautiful illustrations in this book show the front and back of 105 coverlets in the Shein Collection, all made between 1817 and 1869.

INDEX

Page numbers in italics refer to illustrations and captions.

ABOUT THE AUTHORS

Helaine Fendelman brings over 30 years of experience in the art and antiques field to *Instant Expert: Collecting American Folk Art*. She is a certified member and past president of the Appraisers Association of America; her syndicated column, "What is it...What is it Worth?", appears in the Hearst monthly magazine *Country Living*, and she is a syndicated columnist for Scripps Howard News Service. She is a co-host of the PBS television affiliate program, *Treasures In Your Attic* and is a frequent guest appraiser on national television and radio. Ms. Fendelman is currently an instructor for New York University's School of Continuing and Professional Studies, where she teaches in the Appraisal Studies program. Her publications include *All About Appraising, The Definitive Appraisal Handbook: Price It Yourself; Treasures in Your Attic; Tramp Art: A Folk Art Phenomenon; Money in Your Attic—How to Turn Your Furniture, Antiques, Silver and Collectibles Into Cash; Tramp Art: An Itinerant's Folk Art; Silent Companions: Dummy Board Figures of the 17th through 19th Centuries*. She has served as a curator, consultant and lecturer for museums and private organizations throughout the United States. Ms. Fendelman currently runs Helaine Fendelman & Associates, which specializes in appraisals and sales of fine and decorative arts and household items.

Susan Kleckner runs Susan D. Kleckner, LLC, an auction representation, appraisal, private sales and consulting business in American furniture, folk art, and decorative arts. She brings 18 years of academic, museum and marketplace experience to *Instant Expert: Collecting American Folk Art*. Ms. Kleckner's credentials include a B.A. from Yale College (1988) and an M.A. from the University of Delaware's Winterthur Program in Early American Culture (1990). She has worked in the American art collections of Yale University Art Gallery and the Metropolitan Museum of Art and was on the curatorial staff of the Maryland Historical Society. From 1992 to 2002, Ms. Kleckner was a specialist in American decorative arts at Christie's auction house in New York City, where she became Head of the American Folk Art department. During her tenure at Christie's, Kleckner oversaw their most important American folk art sales to date. She also researched and wrote the auction catalog *George Washington: The First Presidential Portrait* (January 2001), regarding a 2-inch portrait miniature of Washington painted in 1789 that set a world auction record for any portrait miniature when it sold for $1.1 million. In addition to running her appraisal, sales and consulting business, Ms. Kleckner is an instructor for New York University's School of Continuing and Professional Studies, where she teaches in the Appraisal Studies program. She presently serves on the Board of the American Decorative Arts Forum of Northern California. She is also an appraiser on WGBH Boston's television program *Antiques Roadshow*. She has written for *Maine Antique Digest* and *Art & Auction* magazine, and lectures extensively on the subjects of American folk art, decorative arts and furniture.